CIVICS 103

CHARTERS THAT FORM AMERICA'S GOVERNMENT

ROGER L. KEMP

authorHOUSE®

AuthorHouse™
1663 Liberty Drive
Bloomington, IN 47403
www.authorhouse.com
Phone: 833-262-8899

Published by AuthorHouse 01/25/2022

ISBN: 978-1-6655-5027-7 (sc)
ISBN: 978-1-6655-5026-0 (e)

Library of Congress Control Number: 2022901448

Print information available on the last page.

DEDICATION

This book is dedicated to Kieran,
The best and the brightest.

CONTENTS

Lesson 4: Model State Government Charter

Lesson 5: Model Federal Government Charter

ACKNOWLEDGEMENTS

Grateful acknowledgements are made to the elected officials, appointed officials, and citizens of those cities that I have worked and lives in during my over a quarter-century public service career on both coasts of the United States.

These states and cities include the following:

- In California – The City of Oakland
                     The City of Seaside
                     The City of Placentia
                     The City of Vallejo

- In New Jersey – The City of Clifton

- In Connecticut – The City of Meriden
                      The Town of Berlin

While I served as a full-time City Manager, I taught public administration courses in graduate programs at universities located close to where I worked as a City Manager. In one or more cases, the school was a distance away, but the courses taught were on-line.

These universities include the following:

- In California – California State University, Fullerton
                     California State University, Long Beach
                     Golden Gate University, San Francisco
                     University of California, Irvine
- In New Jersey – Fairleigh Dickinson University
                     Rutgers University
- In Connecticut – Central Connecticut State University
                      Charter Oak State College
                      Southern Connecticut State University
                      University of Connecticut
                      University of New Haven
- In Minnesota – Capella University

PREFACE

The purpose of this volume is to document and describe each of the model charters for our nation's governments. The resources contained in this book include model government charters for America's city governments, county governments, regional governments, state governments, as well as our nation's federal government. Related Appendices are included at the end of this volume.

The United States of America has the oldest system of federal government in the world. Since the passage of our federal Constitution in 1789, the federal government has gained both power and responsibility. During this time, the states lost much of their original sovereignty given to them when the colonies were initially formed. Much of the shift of power to the federal government is attributable to Supreme Court Chief Justice John Marshall, during the early 19th century, and the federal policies arising from the New Deal of the 1930s, when the problems of the nation were too much for state governments to resolve on their own. This gradual shift of power has also had an influence on lower levels of government, since cities and counties are creatures of the states. Each state's charter and statutes determine the powers and responsibilities of these lower levels of government. Over the years, both the number and types of regional governments have grown in significance. Many of these new regional governments were designed to address recognized urban problems that spill over the artificial man-made political boundaries of our city and county governments. This level of government will continue to grow in the future.

A model charter follows in each chapter. The word *charter* is commonly used to describe the set of laws that forms cities, counties, and regions. On the other hand, the term *constitution* is used when referring to states and the federal government. For ease of reference, the term *charter* denotes those sets of laws forming the basis of all levels of U.S. government. This volume also includes a *Glossary* of commonly used terms and a *National Resource Directory,* which highlights major sources for further research on those subjects contained in this volume. These topics, and the types of information examined in each chapter, are briefly highlighted below.

City Governments

The four basic forms of municipal government in the U.S. include the commission, council manager, mayor-council, and strong mayor plans. The commission plan involves the direct election of legislators who serve as executives to manage the various functions of a municipal organization. This form of government, which merges legislative and administrative functions, because of its obvious shortcomings, remains in only a few small towns in the northeastern portion of the nation. Under the mayor-council plan, the duties of the mayor vary greatly, depending upon the size of the community. The mayor is also elected separately from the city council, and the duties of the mayor vary from municipality to municipality, depending upon a community's charter. Our nation's larger cities are most likely to have the strong mayor form of government. This plan has its obvious advantages and disadvantages, depending upon the qualifications and character of the person selected to serve as mayor. As our nation enters the 21st century, the council-manager plan is the most common form of municipal government, and it is growing at a faster rate than any other form of local government.

For this reason, the *model city charter* sets forth a structure of municipal government that separates policy-making from administration, and insulates the personnel and finance functions from undue political influence. The major topics examined in this charter include the powers of the city government, the role of the city council, and the duties of the city manager. The charter also includes a listing of all departments, offices, and agencies, and delineates in great detail the financial procedures and reporting requirements of the city government. Other important topics in the charter include election procedures and provisions for citizen initiatives and referendums. This charter requires each community to have a Board of Ethics. Provisions are also included for future citizen changes to the charter, always by majority vote of the electorate. These provisions separate legislative and executive powers, and are non-partisan in nature, allowing the appointed professional manager to serve all citizens equally, regardless of their political affiliation.

County Governments

There are three primary types of county government in our nation. They include the commission, council-manager, and the council-elected executive plans. The commission plan allows for the direct election of legislators-administrators, who individually manage the various functions of county government. As with cities, this form of government has declined in popularity over the years, and is seldom used today. Under the council-elected executive plan, the county executive is directly elected by voters and serves as the top administrator of the county government.

This plan can also be good or bad, depending upon the qualifications and character of the person selected to serve as the elected executive. The current trend, like in cities and towns, is towards the council-manager plan. It is the fastest growing form of county government in the country. Under this plan the elected county council appoints the county manager, who is a trained professional. County governments also have some elected department managers, depending upon the requirements of their charter. As is the case with the municipal council-manager plan, this form of government separates policy-making from administration, and insulates the personnel and finance functions of county government from undue political influence. In many county governments, the word "administrator" is used rather than the term "manager."

The *model county charter* mandates the council-manager plan because of its obvious advantages over the other forms of county government. The topics examined in this charter include the powers of the county government, the role of the county council, and the duties of the county manager (or administrator). This charter also includes a listing of all departments, offices, and agencies, and sets forth with specificity the financial procedures and reporting requirements of the county government. Other significant provisions in this charter include provisions for county elections, and requirements for citizen-initiated initiatives and referendums. This charter also requires each county under this plan to have a Board of Ethics. Provisions also contain a process whereby citizens can change their county charter by majority vote. This charter, like the city charter, uses the corporate model of governance [with a chairman and board of directors (chairman and council), a chief executive officer (county manager), and stockholders (citizens)].

Regional Governments

There are six main forms of regional governments in the United States. These include regional planning commissions, councils of government, regional advisory committees, regional allocation agencies, special purpose regional agencies, and home-rule charter regional governments. Regional planning commissions may encompass a single county, multiple counties, multiple municipal jurisdictions, or some combination thereof. Councils of government usually include a number of neighboring cities, contiguous cities and the county they are located in, or adjacent cities and multiple neighboring counties. Regional advisory committees are created by states to oversee the planning function of portions of land within their jurisdiction. Regional allocation agencies are typically responsible for allocating certain federal funds within selected geographic areas, usually substrate in nature. Special purpose regional agencies have the authority to plan and control development in a selected portion of a state. Home-rule charter regional governments are few and far between. While there are some county-city consolidations, and a few state-created regional governments, there is only one regional government in America that has a home-rule charter, and public officials elected by the citizens within the region. This is the Metropolitan Services District in Portland, Oregon. The number of such regional governments will increase in popularity during the coming decades.

For this reason, the citizen-approved charter for this regional planning agency serves as the *model regional government charter* featured in this chapter. The charter for the nation's only home-rule regional government includes provisions that define its name and political boundaries; functions and powers; finances and revenues; form of government; its offices, commissions, and employees; provisions for elections and reapportionment, and power to enact laws (called ordinances). Reapportionment takes place after an "official" government census. The form of government includes the election of a seven (7)-member council, with one member being elected at-large to serve as president of the Metropolitan Council. The president and members of the council all serve four (4)-year terms of office. Voters approved the Metropolitan Services District in 1992. Prior to 1992, the Oregon State Legislature set forth their legal obligations and responsibilities. It is considered by experts as one of the most progressive regional government organizations in the country. The "Metro", as locals usually refer to it, serves over 1.3 million people in a three (3)-county area that contains twenty-four (24) cities in the Portland, Oregon, metropolitan area.

State Governments

Our nation was founded with 13 colonies. When the Founding Fathers wrote the U.S. Constitution in 1787, these colonies became the first states in America. The Founding Fathers believed that more states would want to join the Union in the future, and that each state should have similar powers and structure. Even when the 50th state joined the Union, all states maintained these original characteristics. Each state's government is based on a constitution, and has a republican form of government. No state constitution is allowed to contradict the federal constitution, and each state has three branches of government. These three branches of government include the legislative, executive, and judicial, complete with their separation-of-powers and requirements for checks-and-balances. Most states provide citizens with one or more avenues of direct democracy – the initiative, referendum, or recall. Over the decades, power has shifted from the states to the federal government, especially during times of crisis. The current trend towards the devolution of responsibilities from the federal government to the states is restoring legitimate power to state governments. This trend is significant as our nation enters the third millennium, and likely to continue in the future.

The authority, structure, and responsibilities for each state are embodied in the *model state government charter* (or constitution). The structure of every state government includes provisions for a legislative, judicial, and executive branch of government. This model constitution includes a bill of rights, setting forth the rights of citizens; the powers of the state; and the qualifications to vote and how elections will be held. The roles and responsibilities for the state legislature, executive (governor), and judiciary (court system) are also set forth. The powers of the state to raise revenues and finance government are also established. The organization of local governments (cities and counties) are also included, along with the requirements for municipal and county elections. The state constitution includes civil service safeguards and defines and supports intergovernmental relations. Last, but not least, guidelines are mandated for ways that legislators and citizens can make revisions to their state constitution. The model state constitution clearly sets forth the structure, authority, and responsibilities for the required three (3) levels of state government, and their respective checks-and-balances.

Federal Government

The U.S. Constitution, the charter of the federal government, defines, directly or indirectly, the structure and responsibilities of our central government. According to the Constitution, any power not specifically given to the federal government is a power of the states or of the people. The country has changed tremendously since 1787 when the Founding Fathers wrote the original charter. Circumstances over the years have made it necessary to amend or change the Constitution and to expand the role of the federal government in our intergovernmental system. The original philosophy and concepts contained in the Constitution, however, have not changed over the years even though the federal government has grown in both size and complexity. Political scholars have long recognized the importance of early Supreme Court decisions, primarily during the first quarter of the 19th century, as well as the federal government's policies of the New Deal, during the second quarter of the 20th century, as pivotal periods in redefining the role of the federal government in our nation. The role of the federal government continues to evolve as our nation enters the next century.

The Constitution, our nation's first charter, includes three parts. Part one includes the original charter, and its seven Articles that set forth the organization of the U.S. government, our national election processes, and our government's inherent system of checks-and-balances that still exists today. Part two, called the Bill of Rights, includes Amendments 1 through 10 of the Constitution, which set forth the basic rights of citizens and the numerous safeguards that exist to ensure these rights. The first 10 Amendments were adopted as a unit in 1791. Part three of the Constitution includes some 17 additional Amendments to the Constitution that were ratified during the ensuing two-plus centuries. Amendment 11 was passed in 1798, and Amendment 27 was approved in 1992. Relative to states' rights, the most important of these Amendments is the 14th, which was ratified in 1868. This Amendment placed significant limitations on the powers of the states. It extended the federal protections of the Bill of Rights to citizens under state law, who previously had to look to each state constitution for such rights. The other provision of the 14th Amendment places limits upon the powers of the state and is the guarantee of "equal protection under the law" for all citizens of the United States. The Supreme Court applied this clause in its landmark decision outlawing school segregation (*Brown v. Board of Education of Topeka*, 1954).

The main purpose of this book is to document those government charters that form the basis of each level of government in America now in the early 21st century. After all, the state of our democratic institutions – at all levels of government – is dependent upon the written laws that form the very essence of their existence. Citizens and public officials alike should find this volume useful for a number of reasons. Citizens wishing to improve any level of their government now have access to a set of *model charters* that show the best practices for each level of government. These include forms of organization, election systems, personnel practices, and financial safeguards and reporting requirements, and provisions for direct democracy such as the initiative, referendum, and recall. Public officials also need this type of information as they strive to improve the operations of their own governments to meet the expectations of the citizens they serve. Equally important, as new cities are formed in the unincorporated areas of our nation's counties, citizens and public officials can reference the model municipal charter. This also holds true for new regional governments that may be formed in the years ahead. A model charter now exists that can provide guidelines for similar government agencies.

Most published works on this subject only focus on a single level of government. This is the only volume known to set forth model charters for every level of American government. For this reason, it represents an important codification of knowledge in this field.

While there are thousands of city governments, county governments, and regional governments throughout our nation, there are only 50 state governments and one federal government. The model charters for all of these major levels of government in America are highlighted in this volume.

Lastly, the Appendices at the end of this volume include a glossary of government terms, a history of citizen voting rights in our nation, as well as state and national government resource directories. Closing Appendices include a listing of books by the author, the world travels during his public service career, and some important "final thoughts."

Roger L. Kemp

LESSON ONE

MODEL CITY GOVERNMENT CHARTER

Model City Government Charter

National Civic League

Article I
POWERS OF THE CITY

Section 1.01. Powers of the City.

The city shall have all powers possible for a city to have under the constitution and laws of this state as fully and completely as though they were specifically enumerated in this charter.

Section 1.02. Construction.

The powers of the city under this charter shall be construed liberally in favor of the city, and the specific mention of particular powers in the charger shall not be construed as limiting in any way the general power granted in this article.

Section 1.03. Intergovernmental Relations.

The city may exercise any of its powers or perform any of its functions and may participate in the financing thereof, jointly or in cooperation, by contract or otherwise, with any one or more states or any state civil division or agency, or the United States or any of its agencies.

Article II
CITY COUNCIL

Section 2.01. General Powers and Duties.

All powers of the city shall be vested in the city council, except as otherwise provided by law or this charter, and the council shall provide for the exercise thereof and for the performance of all duties and obligations imposed on the city by law.

Section 2.02. Composition, Eligibility, Election and Terms.

Alternative I: Election At-Large

<u>Form 1</u>

NOTE: This formulation of the at-large council system should be used with the separately elected mayor form of the Council-Manager plan, as found in Alternative I of §2.03. The formulation for use with the form of the Council-Manager plan where the mayor is elected by the council from its membership is found in Form 2.

(a) **Composition.** There shall be a city council composed of the mayor and [even-number] members; the council members shall be elected by the voters of the city at large and the mayor shall be elected as provided in §2.03.

(b) **Eligibility.** Only registered voters of the city shall be eligible to hold the office of council member or mayor.

(c) **Election and Terms.** The regular election of council members shall be held on the _____ of _____ in each odd- [even-] numbered year, in the manner provided by law. At the first election under this charter _____ council members shall be elected; the _____ [one-half the number of council members] candidates receiving the greatest number of votes shall serve for terms of four years, and the _____ [one-half the number of council members] candidates receiving the next greatest number of votes shall serve for terms of two years. Thereafter, all council members shall be elected for four-year terms. The terms of council members shall begin the _____ day of _____ after their election.

NOTE: If staggered terms are not desired, use the following section:

[(c) **Election and Terms.** The regular election of council members shall be held on the _____ day of _____ every _____ years beginning in _____. The terms of council members shall be _____ years beginning the _____ day of _____ after their election.]

Form 2

NOTE: This formulation of the at-large council system should be used with the form of the Council-Manager plan where the mayor is elected by the council from its membership, as found in Alternative II of §2.03. The formulation for use with the separately elected mayor form of the Council-Manager plan is found in Form 1.

(a) **Composition.** There shall be a city council of [odd-number] members elected by the voters of the city at large.

(b) **Eligibility.** Only registered voters of the city shall be eligible to hold the office of council member.

(c) **Election and Terms.** The regular election of council members shall be held on the _____ of _____ in each odd- [even-] numbered year, in the manner provided by law. At the first election under this charter _____ council members shall be elected; the _____ [one-half plus one] candidates receiving the greatest number of votes shall serve for terms of four years, and the _____ [remainder of the council] candidates receiving the next greatest number of votes shall serve for terms of two years. Commencing at the next regular election and at all subsequent elections, all council members shall be elected for four-year terms. The terms of council members shall begin the _____ day of _____ after their election.

NOTE: If staggered terms are not desired, use the following section:

[(c) **Election and Terms.** The regular election of council members shall be held on the _____ day of_____ every _____ years beginning in _____. The terms of council members shall be _____ years beginning the _____ day of _____ after their election.]

Alternative II:
Election At Large with
District Residency Requirement

Form 1

NOTE: This formulation of the at-large council system with district residency requirements should be used with the separately elected mayor form of the Council-Manager plan, as found in Alternative I of §2.03. The formulation for use with the form of the Council-Manager plan where the mayor is elected by the council from its membership is found in Form 2.

(a) **Composition.** There shall be a city council composed of the mayor and [even-number] council members. Not more than one council member shall reside in each of the [even-number] districts provided for in Article VI; all shall be nominated and elected by the voters of the city at large. The mayor shall be elected in accordance with the provision of §2.03.

(b) **Eligibility.** Only registered voters of the city shall be eligible to hold the office of council member or mayor.

(c) **Election and Terms.** The regular election of council members shall be held on the _____ of _____ in each odd- [even-] numbered year, in the manner provided by law. At the first election under this charter _____ council members shall be elected; council members from odd-numbered districts shall serve for terms of two years, and council members from even-numbered districts shall serve for terms of four years. Thereafter, all council members shall serve for terms of four years. The terms of council members shall begin the _____ day of _____ after their election.

NOTE: If staggered terms are not desired, use the following section:

[(c) **Election and Terms.** The regular election of council members shall be held on the _____ day of _____ every _____ years beginning in _____. The terms of council members shall be _____ years beginning the _____ day of _____ after their election.]

Form 2

NOTE: This formulation of the at-large council system with district residence requirements should be used with the form of the Council-Manager plan where the mayor is elected by the council from its membership, as found in Alternative II of §2.03. The formulation for use with the separately elected mayor form of the Council-Manager plan is found in Form 1.

(a) **Composition.** There shall be a city council of [odd-number] members; not more than one shall reside in each of the [odd-number] districts provided for in Article VI. All shall be nominated and elected by the voters of the city at large.

(b) **Eligibility.** Only registered voters of the city shall be eligible to hold the office of council member.

(c) **Election and Terms.** The regular election of council members shall be held on the _____ of _____ in each odd- [even-] numbered year, in the manner provided by law. At the first election under this charter _____ council members shall be elected; the _____ candidates receiving the greatest number of votes shall serve for terms of four years, and the _____ candidates receiving the next greatest number of votes shall serve for terms of two years. Thereafter, all council members shall be elected for four-year terms. The terms of council members shall begin the _____ day of _____ after their election.

NOTE: If staggered terms are not desired, use the following section.

[(c) **Election and Terms.** The regular election of council members shall be held on the _____ day of _____ every _____ years beginning in _____. The terms of council members shall be _____ years beginning the _____ day of _____ after their election.]

**Alternative III: Mixed At-Large and
Single Member District System**

Form 1

NOTE: This formulation of the mixed at-large and single-member district system should be used with Alternative I of §2.03.

(a) **Composition.** There shall be a city council composed of the mayor and [even-number] members. _____ council members shall be nominated and elected by the voters of the city at large, and _____ shall be nominated and elected by the voters of each of the _____ council districts, as provided in Article VI. The mayor shall be elected as provided in §2.02.

(b) **Eligibility.** Only registered voters of the city shall be eligible to hold the office of council member.

(c) **Election and Terms.** The terms of council members shall be _____ years beginning the _____ day of _____ after their election.

Form 2

NOTE: When this formulation of the mixed at-large and single-member district system is used with Alternative II of §2.03 (the form of the Council-Manager plan where the mayor is selected by the council from its membership), it should specify in §2.03 that one of the at-large members shall be designated mayor.

(a) **Composition.** There shall be a city council of [odd-number] members. _____ shall be nominated and elected by the voters of the city at large, and _____ shall be nominated and elected by the voters of each of the _____ council districts, as provided in Article VI.

(b) **Eligibility.** Only registered voters of the city shall be eligible to hold the office of council member.

(c) **Election and Terms.** The terms of council members shall be _____ years beginning the _____ day of _____ after their election.

Alternative IV:
Single-Member District System

NOTE: The single-member district system should be used only where the mayor is elected at large as provided in Alternative I of §2.03 and not where the mayor is elected by and from the council as provided in Alternative II of §2.03.

(a) **Composition.** There shall be a city council composed of the mayor and [even-number] members. One council member shall be nominated and elected by the voters in each of [even-number] council districts. The mayor shall be elected in accordance with the provisions of §2.03.

(b) **Eligibility.** Only registered voters of the city shall be eligible to hold the office of council member or mayor.

(c) **Election and Terms.** The regular election of council members shall be held on the _____ of _____ in each odd- [even-] numbered year, in the manner provided by law. At the first election under this charter _____ council members shall be elected; council members from odd-numbered districts shall serve for terms of two years, and council members from even-numbered districts shall serve for terms of four years. Thereafter, all council members shall serve for terms of four years. The terms of council members shall begin the _____ day of _____ after their election.

NOTE: If staggered terms are not desired, use the following section.

[(c) **Election and Terms.** The regular election of council members shall be held on the _____ day of _____ every _____ years beginning in _____. The terms of council members shall be _____ years beginning the _____ day of _____ after their election.]

Alternative V
(Proportional Representation)

(a) **Composition and Term.** There shall be a city council of [odd-number] members elected by the registered voters of the city at large for a term of _____ years.

(b) **Eligibility.** Only registered voters of the city shall be eligible to hold the office of council member.

(c) **Election.** The regular election of council members shall be held on the _____ of _____ in each odd- [even-] numbered year. The Council shall be elected by proportional representation by the method of the single transferable vote.

Section 2.03. Mayor

Alternative I

At each regular election a mayor shall be elected for a term of _____ [the same term as other council members] years. The mayor shall be a member of the city council and shall preside at meetings of the council, represent the city in intergovernmental relationships, appoint with the advice and consent of the council the members of citizen advisory boards and commissions present an annual state of the city message, and perform other duties specified by the council. The mayor shall be recognized as head of the city government for all ceremonial purposes and by the governor for purposes of military law but shall have no administrative duties. The council shall elect from among its members a deputy mayor who shall act as mayor during the absence or disability of the mayor and, if a vacancy occurs, shall become mayor for the remainder of the unexpired term.

Alternative II

The city council shall elect from among its members officers of the city who shall have the titles of mayor and deputy mayor, each of whom shall serve at the pleasure of the council. The mayor shall preside at meetings of the council, represent the city in intergovernmental relationships, appoint with the advice and consent of the council the members of citizen advisory boards and commissions, present an annual state of the city message, and other duties specified by the council. The mayor shall be recognized as head of the city government for all ceremonial purposes and by the governor for purposes of military law but shall have no administrative duties. The deputy mayor shall act as mayor during the absence or disability of the mayor.

Section 2.04. Compensation; Expenses.

The city council may determine the annual salary of the mayor and council members by ordinance, but no ordinance increasing such salary shall become effective until the date of commencement of the terms of council members elected at the next regular election. The mayor and council members shall receive their actual and necessary expenses incurred in the performance of their duties of office.

Section 2.05. Prohibitions.

(a) **Holding Other Office.** Except where authorized by law, no council member shall hold any other elected public office during the term for which the member was elected to the council. No council member shall hold any other city office or employment during the terms for which the member was elected to the council. No former council member shall hold any compensated appointive office or employment with the city until one year after the expiration of the term for which the member was elected to the council. Nothing in this section shall be construed to prohibit the council from selecting any current or former council member to represent the city on the governing board of any regional or other intergovernmental agency.

(b) **Appointments and Removals.** Neither the city council nor any of its members shall in any manner control or demand the appointment or removal of any city administrative officer or employee whom the city manager or any subordinate of the city manager is empowered to appoint, but the council may express its views and fully and freely discuss with the city manager anything pertaining to appointment and removal of such officers and employees.

(c) **Interference with Administration.** Except for the purpose of inquiries and investigations under §2.09, the council or its members shall deal with city officers and employees who are subject to the direction and supervision of the city manager solely through the city manager, and neither the council nor its members shall give orders to any such officer or employee, either publicly or privately.

Section 2.06. Vacancies; Forfeiture of Office; Filling of Vacancies.

(a) **Vacancies.** The office of a council member shall become vacant upon the member's death, resignation, removal from office or forfeiture of office in any manner authorized by law.

(b) **Forfeiture of Office.** A council member shall forfeit that office if the council member

(1)   lacks at any time during the term of office for which elected any qualification for the office prescribed by this charter or by law,

(2)   violates any express prohibition of this charter,

(3)   is convicted of a crime involving moral turpitude, or

(4)   fails to attend three consecutive regular meetings of the council without being excused by the council.

(c) **Filling of Vacancies.** A vacancy in the city council shall be filled for the remainder of the unexpired term, if any, at the next regular election following not less than 60 days upon the occurrence of the vacancy, but the council by a majority vote of all its remaining members shall appoint a qualified person to fill the vacancy until the person elected to serve the remainder of the unexpired term takes office. If the council fails to do so within 30 days following the occurrence of the vacancy, the election authorities shall call a special election to fill the vacancy, to be held not sooner than 90 days and not later than 120 days following the occurrence of the vacancy, and to be otherwise governed by law. Notwithstanding the requirement in §2.11, if at any time the membership of the council is reduced to less than _____, the remaining members may by majority action appoint additional members to raise the membership to _____.

Section 2.07. Judge of Qualifications.

The city council shall be the judge of the election and qualifications of its members and of the grounds for forfeiture of their office. The council shall have the power to set additional standards of conduct for its members beyond those specified in the charter and may provide for such penalties as it deems appropriate, including forfeiture of office. In order to exercise these powers, the council shall have power to subpoena witnesses, administer oaths and require the production of evidence. A member charged with conduct constituting grounds for forfeiture of office shall be entitled to a public hearing on demand, and notice of such hearing shall be published in one or more newspapers of general circulation in the city at least one week in advance of the hearing. Decisions made by the council under this section shall be subject to judicial review.

Section 2.08. City Clerk.

The city council shall appoint an officer of the city who shall have the title of city clerk. The city clerk shall give notice of council meetings to its members and the public, keep the journal of its proceedings and perform such other duties as are assigned by this charter or by the council or by state law.

Section 2.09. Investigations.

The city council may make investigations into the affairs of the city and the conduct of any city department, office or agency and for this purpose may subpoena witnesses, administer oaths, take testimony and require the production of evidence. Failure or refusal to obey a lawful order issued in the exercise of these powers by the council shall be a misdemeanor punishable by a fine of not more than $_____, or by imprisonment for not more than _____ or both.

Section 2.10. Independent Audit.

The city council shall provide for an independent annual audit of all city accounts and may provide for more frequent audits as it deems necessary. Such audits shall be made by a certified public accountant or firm of such accountants who have no personal interest, direct or indirect, in the fiscal affairs of the city government or any of its officers. The council may, without requiring competitive bids, designate such accountant or firm annually or for a period not exceeding three years, but the designation for any particular fiscal year shall be made no later than 30 days after the beginning of such fiscal year. If the state makes such an audit, the council may accept it as satisfying the requirements of this section.

Section 2.11. Procedure

(a) **Meetings.** The council shall meet regularly at least once in every month at such times and places as the council may prescribe by rule. Special meetings may be held on the call of the mayor or of _____ or more members and, whenever practicable, upon no less than twelve hours notice to each member. Except as allowed by state law, all meetings shall be public; however, the council may recess for the purpose of discussing in a closed or executive session limited to its own membership any matter which would tend to defame or prejudice the character or reputation of any person, if the general subject matter for consideration is expressed in the motion calling for such session and final action on such motion is not taken by the council until the matter is placed on the agenda.

(b) **Rules and Journal.** The city council shall determine its own rules and order of business and shall provide for keeping a journal of its proceedings. This journal shall be a public record.

(c) **Voting.** Voting, except on procedural motions, shall be by roll call and the ayes and nays shall be recorded in the journal. _____ members of the council shall constitute a quorum, but a smaller number may adjourn from time to time and may compel the attendance of absent members in the manner and subject to the penalties prescribed by the rules of the council. No action of the council, except as otherwise provided in the preceding sentence and in §2.06, shall be valid or binding unless adopted by the affirmative vote of _____ or more members of the council.

Section 2.12. Action Requiring an Ordinance.

In addition to other acts required by law or by specific provision of this charter to be done by ordinance, those acts of the city council shall be by ordinance which:

(1) Adopt or amend an administrative code or establish, alter, or abolish any city department, office or agency;

(2) Provide for a fine or other penalty or establish a rule or regulation for violation of which a fine or other penalty is imposed;

(3) Levy taxes;

(4) Grant, renew or extend a franchise;

(5) Regulate the rate charged for its services by a public utility;

(6) Authorize the borrowing of money;

(7) Convey or lease or authorize the conveyance or lease of any lands of the city;

(8) Regulate land use and development; and

(9) Amend or repeal any ordinance previously adopted.

Acts other than those referred to in the preceding sentence may be done either by ordinance or by resolution.

Section 2.13. Ordinances in General.

(a) **Form.** Every proposed ordinance shall be introduced in writing and in the form required for final adoption. No ordinance shall contain more than one subject which shall be clearly expressed in its title. The enacting clause shall be "The city of _____ hereby ordains …." Any ordinance which repeals or amends an existing ordinance or part of the city code shall set out in full the ordinance, sections or subsections to be repealed or amended, and shall indicate matters to be omitted by enclosing it in brackets or by strikeout type and shall indicate new matters by underscoring or by italics.

(b) **Procedure.** An ordinance may be introduced by any member at any regular or special meeting of the council. Upon introduction of any ordinance, the city clerk shall distribute a copy to each council member and to the city manager, shall file a reasonable number of copies in the office of the city clerk and such other public places as the council may designate, and shall publish the ordinance together with a notice setting out the time and place for a public hearing thereon and for its consideration by the council. The public hearing shall follow the publication by at least seven days, may be held separately or in connection with a regular or special council meeting and may be adjourned from time to time; all persons interested shall have an opportunity to be heard. After the hearing the council may adopt the ordinance with or without amendment or reject it, but if it is amended to any matter of substance, the council may not adopt it until the ordinance or its amended sections have been subjected to all the procedures herein before required in the case of a newly introduced ordinance. As soon as practicable after adoption, the clerk shall have the ordinance and a notice of its adoption published and available at a reasonable price.

(c) **Effective Date.** Except as otherwise provided in this charter, every adopted ordinance shall become effective at the expiration of 30 days after adoption or at any later date specified therein.

(d) **"Publish" Defined.** As used in this section, the term "publish" means to print in one or more newspapers of general circulation in the city: (1) The ordinance or a brief summary thereof, and

(2) the places where copies of it have been filed and the times when they are available for public inspection and purchase at a reasonable price.

Section 2.14. Emergency Ordinances.

To meet a public emergency affecting life, health, property or the public peace, the city council may adopt one or more emergency ordinances, but such ordinances may not levy taxes, grant renew or extend a franchise, regulate the rate charged by any public utility for its services or authorize the borrowing of money except as provided in §5.07(b). An emergency ordinance shall be introduced in the form and manner prescribed for ordinances generally, except that it shall be plainly designated as an emergency ordinance and shall contain, after the enacting clause, a declaration stating that an emergency exists and describing it in clear and specific terms. An emergency ordinance may be adopted with or without amendment or rejected at the meeting at which it is introduced, but the affirmative vote of at least _____ members shall be required for adoption. After its adoption the ordinance shall be published and printed as prescribed for other adopted ordinances. It shall become effective upon adoption or at such later time as it may specify. Every emergency ordinance except one made pursuant to §5.07(b) shall automatically stand repealed as of the 61st day following the date on which it was adopted, but this shall not prevent reenactment of the ordinance in the manner specified in this section if the emergency still exists. An emergency ordinance may also be repealed by adoption of a repealing ordinance in the same manner specified in this section for adoption of emergency ordinances.

Section 2.15. Codes of Technical Regulations.

The city council may adopt any standard code of technical regulations by reference thereto in an adopting ordinance. The procedure and requirements governing such an adopting ordinance shall be as prescribed for ordinances generally except that:

(1)   The requirements of §2.13 for distribution and filing of copies of the ordinance shall be construed to include copies of the code of technical regulations as well as of the adopting ordinance, and

(2)   A copy of each adopted code of technical regulations as well as of the adopting ordinance shall be authenticated and recorded by the city clerk pursuant to §2.16(a).

Copies of any adopted code of technical regulations shall be made available by the city clerk for distribution or for purchase at a reasonable price.

Section 2.16. Authentication and Recording; Codification; Printing.

(a) **Authentication and Recording.** The city clerk shall authenticate by signing and shall record in full in a properly indexed book kept for the purpose all ordinances and resolutions adopted by the city council.

(b) **Codification.** Within three years after adoption of this charter and at least every ten years thereafter, the city council shall provide for the preparation of a general codification of all city ordinances and resolutions having the force and effect of law. The general codification shall be adopted by the council by ordinance and shall be published promptly in bound or loose-leaf form, together with this charter and any amendments thereto, pertinent provisions of the constitution and other laws of the state of _____, and such codes of technical regulations and other rules and regulations as the council may specify. This compilation shall be known and cited officially as the _____ city code. Copies of the code shall be furnished to city officers, placed in libraries and public offices for free public reference and made available for purchase by the public at a reasonable price fixed by the council.

(c) **Printing of Ordinances and Resolutions.** The city council shall cause each ordinance and resolution having the force and effect of law and each amendment to this charter to be printed promptly following its adoption, and the printed ordinances, resolutions and charter amendments shall be distributed or sold to the public at reasonable prices as fixed by the council. Following publication of the first _____ City Code and at all times thereafter, the ordinances, resolutions and charter amendments shall be printed in substantially the same style as the code currently in effect and shall be suitable in form for integration therein. The council shall make such further arrangements as it deems desirable with respect to reproduction and distribution of any current changes in or additions to the provisions of the constitution and other laws of the state of _____, or the codes of technical regulations and other rules and regulations included in the code.

Article III
CITY MANAGER

Section 3.01. Appointment; Qualifications; Compensation.
The city council by a majority vote of its total membership shall appoint a city manager for an indefinite term and fix the manager's compensation. The city manager shall be appointed solely on the basis of executive and administrative qualifications. The manager need not be a resident of the city or state at the time of appointment but may reside outside the city while in office only with the approval of the council.

Section 3.02. Removal.
The city manager may be suspended by a resolution approved by the majority of the total membership of the city council which shall set forth the reasons for suspension and proposed removal. A copy of such resolution shall be served immediately upon the city manager. The city manager shall have fifteen days in which to reply thereto in writing, and upon request, shall be afforded a public hearing, which shall occur not earlier than ten days nor later than fifteen days after such hearing is requested. After the public hearing, if one be requested, and after full consideration, the city council by a majority vote of its total membership may adopt a final resolution of removal. The city manager shall continue to receive full salary until the effective date of a final resolution of removal.

Section 3.03. Acting City Manager.

By letter filed with the city clerk, the city manager shall designate a city officer or employee to exercise the powers and perform the duties of city manager during the manager's temporary absence or disability. The city council may revoke such designation at any time and appoint another officer of the city to serve until the city manager returns.

Section 3.04. Powers and Duties of the City Manager.

The city manager shall be the chief administrative officer of the city, responsible to the Council for the administration of all city affairs placed in the manager's charge by or under this charter. The city manager shall:

(1) Appoint and, when necessary for the good of the service, suspend or remove all city employees and appointive administrative officers provided for, by or under this charter, except as otherwise provided by law, this charter or personnel rules adopted pursuant to this charter. The city manager may authorize any administrative officer subject to the manager's direction and supervision to exercise these powers with respect to subordinances in that officer's department, office or agency;

(2) Direct and supervise the administration of all departments, offices and agencies of the city, except as otherwise provided by this charter or by law;

(3) Attend all city council meetings. The city manager shall have the right to take part in discussion but shall not vote;

(4) See that all laws, provisions of this charter and acts of the city council, subject to enforcement by the city manager or by officers subject to the manager's direction and supervision, are faithfully executed;

(5) Prepare and submit the annual budget and capital program to the city council;

(6) Submit to the city council and make available to the public a complete report on the finances and administrative activities of the city as of the end of each fiscal year;

(7) Make such other reports as the city council may require concerning the operations of city departments, offices and agencies subject to the city manager's direction and supervision;

(8) Keep the city council fully advised as to the financial condition and future needs of the city;

(9) Make recommendations to the city council concerning the affairs of the city;

(10) Provide staff support services for the mayor and council members; and

(11) Perform such other duties as are specified in this charter or may be required by the city council.

Article IV
DEPARTMENTS, OFFICES AND AGENCIES

Section 4.01. General Provisions.

(a) **Creation of Departments.** The city council may establish city departments, offices or agencies in addition to those created by this charter and may prescribe the functions of all departments, offices and agencies, except that no function assigned by this charter to a particular department, office or agency may be discontinued or, unless this charter specifically so provides, assigned to any other.

(b) **Direction by City Manager.** All departments, offices and agencies under the direction and supervision of the city manager shall be administered by an officer appointed by and subject to the direction and supervision of the manager. With the consent of council, the city manager may serve as the head of one or more such departments, offices or agencies or may appoint one person as the head of two or more of them.

Section 4.02. Personnel System.
(a) **Merit Principle.** All appointments and promotions of city officers and employees shall be made solely on the basis of merit and fitness demonstrated by a valid and reliable examination or other evidence of competence.

(b) **Merit System.** Consistent with all applicable federal and state laws the city council shall provide by ordinance for the establishment, regulation and maintenance of a merit system governing personnel policies necessary to effective administration of the employees of the city's departments, offices and agencies, including but not limited to classification and pay plans, examinations, force reduction, removals, working conditions, provisional and exempt appointments, in-service training, grievances and relationships with employee organizations.

Section 4.03. Legal Officer.

Alternative I

There shall be a legal officer of the city appointed by the city manager as provided in §4.01(b). The legal officer shall serve as chief legal adviser to the city council, the manager and all city departments, offices and agencies, shall represent the city in all legal proceedings and shall perform any other duties prescribed by state law, by this charter or by ordinance.

Alternative II

There shall be a legal officer of the city appointed by the city manager subject to confirmation by the city council. The legal officer shall serve as chief legal adviser to the council, the manager and all city departments, offices and agencies, shall represent the city in all legal proceedings and shall perform any other duties prescribed by state law, by this charter or by ordinance.

Alternative III

There shall be a legal officer of the city appointed by the city council. The legal officer shall serve as chief legal adviser to the council, the city manager and all city departments, offices and agencies, shall represent the city in all legal proceedings and shall perform any other duties prescribed by state law, by this charter or by ordinance.

Section 4.04. Planning.

Consistent with all applicable federal and state laws with respect to land use, development and environmental protection, the city council shall:

(1)   Designate an agency or agencies to carry out the planning function and such decision-making responsibilities as may be specified by ordinance;

(2)   Adopt a comprehensive plan and determine to what extent zoning and other land use control ordinances must be consistent with the plan; and

(3)   Adopt development regulations, to be specified by ordinance, to implement the plan.

Article V
FINANCIAL PROCEDURES

Section 5.01. Fiscal Year.

The fiscal year of the city shall begin on the first day of _____ and end on the last day of _____.

Section 5.02. Submission of Budget and Budget Message.

On or before the _____ day of each year, the city manager shall submit to the city council a budget for the ensuing fiscal year and an accompanying message.

Section 5.03. Budget Message.

The city manager's message shall explain the budget both in fiscal terms and in terms of the work programs. It shall outline the proposed financial policies of the city for the ensuing fiscal year, describe the important features of the budget, indicate any major changes from the current year in financial policies, expenditures, and revenues together with the reasons for such changes, summarize the city's debt position and include such other material as the city manager deems desirable.

Section 5.04. Budget.

The budget shall provide a complete financial plan of all city funds and activities for the ensuing fiscal year and, except as required by law or this charter, shall be in such form as the city manager deems desirable or the city council may require. The budget shall begin with a clear general summary of its contents; shall show in detail all estimate income, indicating the proposed property tax levy, and all proposed expenditures, including debt service, for the ensuing fiscal year; and shall be so arranged as to show comparative figures for actual and estimated income and expenditures of the current fiscal year and actual income and expenditures of the preceding fiscal year. It shall indicate in separate sections:

(1)   The proposed goals and objectives and expenditures for current operations during the ensuing fiscal year, detailed for each fund by organization unit, and program, purpose or activity, and the method of financing such expenditures;

(2)   Proposed capital expenditures during the ensuing fiscal year, detailed for each fund by organization unit when practicable, and the proposed method of financing each such capital expenditure; and

(3)   The anticipated income and expense and profit and loss for the ensuing year for each utility or other enterprise fund operated by the city.

For any fund, the total of proposed expenditures shall not exceed the total of estimated income plus carried forward fund balance, exclusive of reserves.

Section 5.05. City Council Action on Budget.

(a) **Notice and hearing.** The city council shall publish in one or more newspapers of general circulation in the city the general summary of the budget and a notice stating:

(1)   The times and places where copies of the message and budget are available for inspection by the public, and

(2)   The time and place, not less than two weeks after such publication, for a public hearing on the budget.

(b) **Amendment Before Adoption.** After the public hearing, the city council may adopt the budget with or without amendment. In amending the budget, it may add or increase programs or amounts and may delete or decrease any programs or amounts, except expenditures required by law or for debt service or for an estimated cash deficit, provided that no amendment to the budget shall increase the authorized expenditures to an amount greater than total estimated income.

(c) **Adoption.** The city council shall adopt the budget on or before the _____ day of the _____ month of the fiscal year currently ending. If it fails to adopt the budget by this date, the budget proposed by the city manager shall go into effect.

Section 5.06. Appropriation and Revenue Ordinances.

To implement the adopted budget, the city council shall adopt, prior to the beginning of the ensuing fiscal year:

(a)   an appropriation ordinance making appropriations by department or major organizational unit and authorizing a single appropriation for each program or activity;

(b)   a tax levy ordinance authorizing the property tax levy or levies and setting the tax rate or rates; and

(c)   any other ordinances required to authorize new revenues or to amend the rates or other features of existing taxes or other revenue sources.

Section 5.07. Amendments after Adoption.

(a) **Supplemental Appropriations.** If during the fiscal year the city manager certifies that there are available for appropriation revenues in excess of those estimated in the budget, the city council by ordinance may make supplemental appropriations for the year up to the amount of such excess.

(b) **Emergency Appropriations.** To meet a public emergency affecting life, health, property or the public peace, the city council may make emergency appropriations. Such appropriations may be made by emergency ordinance in accordance with the provisions of §2.14. To the extent that there are no available unappropriated revenues or a sufficient fund balance to meet such appropriations, the council may by such emergency ordinance authorize the issuance of emergency notes, which may be renewed from time to time, but the emergency notes and renewals of any fiscal year shall be paid not later than the last day of the fiscal year next succeeding that in which the emergency appropriation was made.

(c) **Reduction of Appropriations.** If at any time during the fiscal year it appears probable to the city manager that the revenues or fund balances available will be insufficient to finance the expenditures for which appropriations have been authorized, the manager shall report to the city council without delay, indicating the estimated amount of the deficit, any remedial action taken by the manager and recommendations as to any other steps to be taken. The council shall then take such further action as it deems necessary to prevent or reduce any deficit and for that purpose it may by ordinance reduce one or more appropriations.

(d) **Transfer of Appropriations.** At any time during the fiscal year the city council may by resolution transfer part or all of the unencumbered appropriation balance from one department or major organizational unit to the appropriation for other departments or major organizational units. The manager may transfer part or all of any unencumbered appropriation balances among programs within a department or organizational unit and shall report such transfers to the council in writing in a timely manner.

(e) **Limitation; Effective Date.** No appropriation for debt service may be reduced or transferred, and no appropriation may be reduced below any amount required by law to be appropriated or by more than the amount of the unencumbered balance thereof. The supplemental and emergency appropriations and reduction or transfer of appropriations authorized by this section may be made effective immediately upon adoption.

Section 5.08. Lapse of Appropriations.

Every appropriation, except an appropriation for a capital expenditure, shall lapse at the close of the fiscal year to the extent that it has not been expended or encumbered. An appropriation for a capital expenditure shall continue in force until expended, revised or repealed; the purpose of any such appropriation shall be deemed abandoned if three years pass without any disbursement from or encumbrance of the appropriation.

Section 5.09. Administration of the Budget.

The city council shall provide by ordinance the procedures for administering the budget.

Section 5.10. Overspending of Appropriations Prohibited.

No payment shall be made or obligation incurred against any allotment or appropriation except in accordance with appropriations duly made and unless the city manager or his designee first certifies that there is a sufficient unencumbered balance in such allotment or appropriation and that sufficient funds therefrom are or will be available to cover the claim or meet the obligation when it becomes due and payable. Any authorization of payment or incurring of obligation in violation of the provisions of this charter shall be void and any payment so made illegal. A violation of this provision shall be cause for removal of any officer who knowingly authorized or made such payment or incurred such obligation. Such officer may also be liable to the city for any amount so paid. Except where prohibited by law, however, nothing in this charter shall be construed to prevent the making or authorizing of payments or making of contracts for capital improvements to be financed wholly or partly by the issuance of bonds or to prevent the making of any contract or lease providing for payments beyond the end of the fiscal year, but only if such action is made or approved by ordinance.

Section 5.11. Capital Program.

(a) **Submission to City Council.** The city manager shall prepare and submit to the city council a five- [six-] year capital program no later than the final date for submission of the budget.

(b) **Contents.** The capital program shall include:

(1)   A clear general summary of its contents;

(2)   A list of all capital improvements and other capital expenditures which are proposed to be undertaken during the five [six] fiscal years next ensuing, with appropriate supporting information as to the necessity for each;

(3)   Cost estimates and recommended time schedule for each improvement or other capital expenditure;

(4)   Method of financing, upon which each capital expenditure is to be reliant; and

(5)   The estimated annual cost of operating and maintaining the facilities to be constructed or acquired.

The above shall be revised and extended each year with regard to capital improvements still pending or in process of construction or acquisition.

Section 5.12. City Council Action on Capital Program.

(a) **Notice and Hearing.** The city council shall publish in one or more newspapers of general circulation in the city the general summary of the capital program and a notice stating:

(1)   The times and places where copies of the capital program are available for inspection by the public, and

(2)   The time and place, not less than two weeks after such publication, for a public hearing on the capital program.

(b) **Adoption.** The city council by resolution shall adopt the capital program with or without amendment after the public hearing and on or before the _____ day of the _____ month of the current fiscal year.

Section 5.13. Public Records.

Copies of the budget, capital program and appropriation and revenue ordinances shall be public records and shall be made available to the public at suitable places in the city.

Article VI
ELECTIONS

Section 6.01. City Elections.

(a) **Regular Elections.** The regular city election shall be held at the time established by state law.

(b) **Registered Voter defined.** All citizens legally registered under the constitution and laws of the state of _____ to vote in the city shall be registered voters of the city within the meaning of this charter.

(c) **Conduct of Elections.** The provisions of the general election laws of the state of _____ shall apply to elections held under this charter. All elections provided for by the charter shall be conducted by the election authorities established by law. Candidates shall run for office without party designation. For the conduct of city elections, for the prevention of fraud in such elections and for the recount of ballots in cases of doubt or fraud, the city council shall adopt ordinances consistent with law and this charter, and the election authorities may adopt further regulations consistent with law and this charter and the ordinances of the council. Such ordinances and regulations pertaining to elections shall be publicized in the manner of city ordinances generally.

Section 6.02. Council Districts; Adjustment of Districts. (for use with Alternatives II, III and IV of §2.02)

(a) **Number of Districts.** There shall be _____ city council districts.

(b) **Districting Commission; Composition; Appointment; Terms; Vacancies; Compensation.**

(1) There shall be a districting commission consisting of five members. No more than two commission members may belong to the same political party. The city council shall appoint four members. These four members shall, with the affirmative vote of at least three, choose the fifth member who shall be chairman.

(2) No member of the commission shall be employed by the city or hold any other elected or appointed position in the city.

(3) The city council shall appoint the commission no later than one year and five months before the first general election of the city council after each federal decennial census. The commission's term shall end upon adoption of a districting plan, as set forth in §6.02(c).

(4) In the event of a vacancy on the Commission by death, resignation or otherwise, the city council shall appoint a anew member enrolled in the same political party from which his or her predecessor was selected, to serve the balance of the term remaining.

(5) No member of the districting commission shall be removed from office by the city council except for cause and upon notice and hearing.

(6) The members of the commission shall serve without compensation except that each member shall be allowed actual and necessary expenses to be audited in the same manner as other city charges.

(7) The commission may hire or contract for necessary staff assistance and may require agencies of city government to provide technical assistance. The commission shall have a budget as provided by the city council.

(c) **Powers and Duties of the Commission; Hearings, Submissions and Approval of Plan.**

(1) Following each decennial census, the commission shall consult the city council and shall prepare a plan for dividing the city into districts for the election of council members. In preparing the plan, the commission shall be guided by the criteria set forth in §6.02(d). The report on the plan shall include a map and description of districts recommended.

(2) The commission shall hold one or more public hearings not less than one month before it submits the plan to the city council. The commission shall make its plan available to the public for inspection and comment not less than one month before its public hearing.

(3) The commission shall submit its plan to the city council not less than one year before the first general election of the city council after each decennial census.

(4) The plan shall be deemed adopted by the city council unless disapproved within three weeks by the vote of the majority of all members of the city council. If the city council fails to adopt the plan, it shall return the plan to the commission with its objections, and with the objections of individual members of the council.

(5) Upon rejection of its plan, the commission shall prepare a revised plan and shall submit such revised plan to the city council no later than nine months before the first general election of the city council after the decennial census. Such revised plan shall be deemed adopted by the city council unless disapproved within two weeks by the vote of two-thirds of all of the members of the city council and unless, by a vote of two-thirds of all of its members, the city council votes to file a petition in the _____ Court, _____ County, for a determination that the plan fails to meet the requirements of this charter. The city council shall file its petition no later than ten days after its disapproval of the plan. Upon a final determination upon appeal, if any, that the plan meets the requirements of this charter, the plan shall be deemed adopted by the city council and the commission shall deliver the plan to the city clerk. The plan delivered to the city clerk shall include a map and description of the districts.

(6) If in any year population figures are not available at least one year and five months before the first general election following the decennial census, the city council may by local law shorten the time period provided for districting commission action in subsections (2), (3), (4) and (5) of this section.

(d) **Districting Plan; Criteria.** In preparation of its plan for dividing the city into districts for the election of council members, the commission shall apply the following criteria which, to the extent practicable, shall be applied and given priority in the order in which they are herein set forth.

(1) Districts shall be equal in population except where deviations from equality result from the application of the provisions hereinafter set forth, but no such deviation may exceed five percent of the average population for all city council districts according to the figures available from the most recent census.

(2) Districts shall consist of contiguous territory; but land areas separated by waterways shall not be included in the same district unless said waterways are traversed by highway bridges, tunnels or regularly scheduled ferry services both termini of which are within the district, except that, population permitting, islands not connected to the mainland or to other islands by a bridge, tunnel or regular ferry services shall be included in the same district as the nearest land area within the city and, where such subdivisions exist, within the same ward or equivalent subdivisions described in subdivision (5), below.

(3) No city block shall be divided in the formation of districts.

(4) In cities whose territory encompasses more than one county or portions of more than one county, the number of districts which include territory in more than one county shall be as small as possible.

21

(5) In the establishment of districts within cities whose territory is divided into wards or equivalent subdivisions whose boundaries have remained substantially unaltered for at least fifteen years, the number of such wards or equivalent subdivisions whose territory is divided among more than one district shall be as small as possible.

(6) Consistent with the foregoing provisions, the aggregate length of all district boundaries shall be as short as possible.

(e) **Effect of Enactment.** The new city council districts and boundaries as of the date of enactment shall supersede previous council districts and boundaries for all purposes of the next regular city election, including nominations. The new districts and boundaries shall supersede previous districts and boundaries for all other purposes as of the date on which all council members elected at that regular city election take office.

[**Section 6.03. Initiative and Referendum.**

The powers of initiative and referendum are hereby reserved to the electors of the city. The provisions of the election law of the state of _____, as they currently exist or may hereafter be amended or superseded, shall govern the exercise of the powers of initiative and referendum under this charter.]

NOTE: Section 6.03 is in brackets because not all states provide for the initiative and referendum and it is possible that not all cities within the states that do provide for it will choose to include the option in their charters.

Article VII
GENERAL PROVISIONS

Section 7.01. Conflicts of Interest; Board of Ethics.
(a) **Conflicts of Interest.** The use of public office for private gain is prohibited. The city council shall implement this prohibition by ordinance. Regulations to this end shall include but not be limited to: acting in an official capacity on matters in which the official has a private financial interest clearly separate from that of the general public; the acceptance of gifts and other things of value; acting in a private capacity on matters dealt with as a public official, the use of confidential information; and appearances by city officials before other city agencies on behalf of private interests. This ordinance shall provide for reasonable public disclosure of finances by officials with major decision-making authority over monetary expenditures and contractual matters and, insofar as permissible under state law, shall provide for fines and imprisonment for violations.

(b) **Board of Ethics.** The city council shall, by ordinance, establish an independent board of ethics to administer and enforce the conflict of interest and financial disclosure ordinances. No member of the board may hold elective or appointed office under the city or any other government or hold any political party office. Insofar as possible under state law, the city council shall authorize the board to issue binding advisory opinions, conduct investigations on its own initiative and on referral or complaint, refer cases for prosecution, impose administrative fines, and to hire independent counsel. The city council shall appropriate sufficient funds to the board of ethics to enable it to perform the duties assigned to it.

Section 7.02. Prohibitions.
(a) Activities Prohibited.

(1) No person shall be appointed to or removed from, or in any way favored or discriminated against with respect to any city position or appointive city administrative office because of race, gender, age, handicap, religion, country of origin or political affiliation.

(2) No person shall willfully make any false statement, certificate, mark, rating or report in regard to any test, certification or appointment under the provisions of this charter or the rules and regulations made thereunder, or in any manner commit or attempt to commit any fraud preventing the impartial execution of such provisions, rules and regulations.

(3) No person who seeks appointment or promotion with respect to any city position or appointive city administrative office shall directly or indirectly give, render or pay any money, service or other valuable thing to any person for or in connection with his or her test, appointment, proposed appointment, promotion or proposed promotion.

(4) No person shall knowingly or willfully solicit or assist in soliciting any assessment, subscription or contribution for any political party or political purpose to be used in conjunction with any city election from any city employee.

(5) No city employee shall knowingly or willfully make, solicit or receive any contribution to the campaign funds of any political party or committee to be used in a city election or to campaign funds to be used in support of or opposition to any candidate for election to city office or city ballot issue. Further, no city employee shall knowingly or willfully participate in any aspect of any political campaign on behalf of or opposition to any candidate for city office. This section shall not be construed to limit any person's right to exercise rights as a citizen to express opinions or to cast a vote nor shall it be construed to prohibit any person from active participation in political campaigns at any other level of government.

(b) **Penalties.** Any person convicted of a violation of this section shall be ineligible for a period of five years following such conviction to hold any city office or position and, if an officer or employee of the city, shall immediately forfeit his or her office or position. The city council shall establish by ordinance such further penalties as it may deem appropriate.

Article VIII
CHARTER AMENDMENT

Section 8.01. Proposal of Amendment.

Amendments to this charter may be framed and proposed:

(a) In the manner provided by law, or
(b) By ordinance of the city council containing the full text of the proposed amendment and effective upon adoption, or
(c) By report of a charter commission created by ordinance, or
(d) By the voters of the city.

When any five qualified voters initiate proceedings to amend the charter by filing with the city clerk an affidavit stating they will constitute the petitioners' committee and be responsible for circulating the petition and filing it in proper form, stating their names and addresses and specifying the address to which all notices to the committee are to be sent, and setting out in full the proposed charter amendment. Promptly after the affidavit of the petitioners' committee is filed the clerk shall issue the appropriate petition blanks to the petitioners' committee. The petitions shall contain or have attached thereto throughout their circulation the full text of the proposed charter amendment and must be signed by registered voters of the city in the number of at least twenty percent of the total number of registered voters at the last regular city election. The petitioners' committee may withdraw the petition at any time before the fifteenth day immediately preceding the day scheduled for the city vote on the amendment.

Section 8.02. Election.

Upon delivery to the city election authorities of the report of a charter commission or delivery by the city clerk of an adopted ordinance proposing an amendment pursuant to §8.01(b) or a petition finally determined sufficient proposing an amendment pursuant to §8.01(d), the election authorities shall submit the proposed amendment to the voters of the city at an election. Such election shall be announced by a notice containing the complete text of the proposed amendment and published in one or more newspapers of general circulation in the city at least 30 days prior to the date of the election. If the amendment is proposed by petition, the amendment may be withdrawn at any time prior to the fifteenth day preceding the day scheduled for the election by filing with the city clerk a request for withdrawal signed by at least four members of the petitioners' committee. The election shall be held not less than 60 and not more than 120 days after the adoption of the ordinance or report or the final determination of sufficiency of the petition proposing the amendment. If no regular election is to be held within that period, the city council shall provide for a special election on the proposed amendment; otherwise, the holding of a special election shall be as specified in the state election law.

Section 8.03. Adoption of Amendment.

If a majority of the registered voters of the city voting upon a proposed charter amendment vote in favor of it, the amendment shall become effective at the time fixed in the amendment or, if no time is therein fixed, 30 days after its adoption by the voters.

Article IX

TRANSITION/SEPARABLITY PROVISION

Section 9.01. Officers and Employees.

(a) **Rights and Privileges Preserved.** Nothing in this charter except as otherwise specifically provided shall affect or impair the rights or privileges of persons who are city officers or employees at the time of its adoption.

(b) **Continuance of Office or Employment.** Except as specifically provided by this charter, if at the time this charter takes full effect a city administrative officer or employee holds any office or position which is or can be abolished by or under this charter, he or she shall continue in such office or position until the taking effect of some specific provision under this charter directing that he or she vacate the office or position.

(c) **Personnel System.** An employee holding a city position at the time this charter takes full effect, who was serving in that same or a comparable position at the time of its adoption, shall not be subject to competitive tests as a condition of continuance in the same position but in all other respects shall be subject to the personnel system provided for in §4.02.

Section 9.02. Departments, Offices and Agencies.

(a) **Transfer of Powers.** If a city department, office or agency is abolished by this charter, the powers and duties given it by law shall be transferred to the city department, office or agency designated in this charter or, if the charter makes no provision, designated by the city council.

(b) **Property and Records.** All property, records and equipment of any department, office or agency existing when this charter is adopted shall be transferred to the department, office or agency assuming its powers and duties, but, in the event that the powers or duties are to be discontinued or divided between units or in the event that any conflict arises regarding a transfer, such property, records or equipment shall be transferred to one or more departments, offices or agencies designated by the city council in accordance with this charter.

Section 9.03. Pending Matters.

All rights, claims, actions, orders, contracts and legal administrative proceedings shall continue except as modified pursuant to the provisions of this charter and in each case shall be maintained, carried on or dealt with by the city department, office or agency appropriate under this charter.

Section 9.04. State and Municipal Laws.

(a) **In General.** All city ordinances, resolutions, orders and regulations which are in force when this charter becomes fully effective are repealed to the extent that they are inconsistent or interfere with the effective operation of this charter or of ordinances or resolutions adopted pursuant thereto. To the extent that the constitution and laws of the state of _____ permit, all laws relating to or affecting this city or its agencies, officers or employees which are in force when this charter becomes fully effective are superseded to the extent that they are inconsistent or interfere with the effective operation of this charter or of ordinances or resolutions adopted pursuant thereto.

(b) **Specific Provisions.** Without limitation of the general operation of subjection (a) or of the number or nature of the provisions to which it applies:

    (1)   The following laws and parts of laws generally affecting counties or city agencies, officers or employees are inapplicable to the city of _____ or its agencies, officers or employees: [enumeration]

    (2)   The following public local laws relating to the city of _____ are superseded: [enumeration]

    (3)   The following ordinances, resolutions, orders and regulations of _____ [former city governing body] are repealed: [enumeration]

Section 9.05. Schedule.

(a) **First Election.** At the time of its adoption, this charter shall be in effect to the extent necessary in order that the first election of members of the city council may be conducted in accordance with the provisions of this charter. The first election shall be held on the _____ of _____. The _____ [city officials to be designated] shall prepare and adopt temporary regulations applicable only to the first election and designed to insure its proper conduct and to prevent fraud and provide for recount of ballots in cases of doubt or fraud.

(b) **Time of Taking Full Effect.** The charter shall be in full effect for all purposes on and after the date and time of the first meeting of the newly elected city council provided in §9.05(c).

(c) **First Council Meeting.** On the _____ of _____ following the first election of city council members under this charter, the newly elected members of the council shall meet at _____ [time] at _____ [place]:

    (1)   For the purpose of electing the [mayor and] deputy mayor, appointing or considering the appointment of a city manager or acting city manager, and choosing, if it so desires, one of its members to act as temporary clerk pending appointment of a city clerk pursuant to §2.08; and

        Note: Omit bracketed words if Section 2.03, Alternative I is used.

(2)   For the purpose of adopting ordinances and resolutions necessary to effect the transition of government under this charter and to maintain effective city government during that transition.

(d) **Temporary Ordinances.** In adopting ordinances as provided in §9.05(c), the city council shall follow the procedures prescribed in Article II, except that at its first meeting or any meeting held within 60 days thereafter, the council may adopt temporary ordinances to deal with cases in which there is an urgent need for prompt action in connection with the transition of government and in which the delay incident to the appropriate ordinance procedure would probably cause serious hardship or impairment of effective city government. Every temporary ordinance shall be plainly labelled as such but shall be introduced in the form and manner prescribed for ordinances generally. A temporary ordinance may be considered and may be adopted with or without amendment or rejected at the meeting at which it is introduced. After adoption of a temporary ordinance, the council shall cause it to be printed and published as prescribed for other adopted ordinances. A temporary ordinance shall become effective upon adoption or at such later time preceding automatic repeal under this subsection as it may specify, and the referendum power shall not extend to any such ordinance. Every temporary ordinance, including any amendments made thereto after adoption, shall automatically stand repealed as of the 91st day following the date on which it was adopted, renewed or otherwise continued except by adoption in the manner prescribed in Article II for ordinances of the kind concerned.

(e) **Initial Expenses.** The initial expenses of the city council, including the expense of recruiting a city manager, shall be paid by the city on vouchers signed by the council chairman.

(f) **Initial Salary of Mayor and Council Members.** The chairman of the council shall receive an annual salary in the amount of $_____$ and each other council member in the amount of $_____$, until such amount is changed by the council in accordance with the provisions of this charter.

Section 9.06. Separability.
If any provision of this charter is held invalid, the other provisions of the charter shall not be affected thereby. If the application of the charter or any of its provisions to any person or circumstance is held invalid, the application of the charter and its provisions to other persons or circumstances shall not be affected thereby.

— — — —

Editor's Note: A complete copy of this document may be obtained from the National Civic League, 1445 Market Street, Suite 300, Denver, Colorado 80202-1717.

LESSON TWO

MODEL COUNTY GOVERNMENT CHARTER

Model County Government Charter

National Civic League

Article I
POWERS OF THE COUNTY

Section 1.01. Powers of the County.

The county shall have all powers possible for a county to have under the constitution and laws of this state as fully and completely as though they were specifically enumerated in this charter.

Section 1.02. Construction.

The powers of the county under this charter shall be construed liberally in favor of the county, and the specific mention of particular powers in the charter shall not be construed as limiting in any way the general power granted in this article.

Section 1.03. Intergovernmental Relations.

The county may exercise any of its powers or perform any of its functions and may participate in the financing thereof, jointly or in cooperation, by contract or otherwise, with any one or more states or any state civil division or agency, or the United States or any of its agencies.

Article II
COUNTY COUNCIL

Section 2.01. General Powers and Duties.

All powers of the county shall be vested in the county council, except as otherwise provided by law or this charter, and the council shall provide for the exercise thereof and for the performance of all duties and obligations imposed on the county by law.

Section 2.02. Composition, Eligibility, Election and Terms.

Alternative I: Election at Large

(a) **Composition.** There shall be a county council of [odd-number] members elected by the voters of the county at large.

(b) **Eligibility.** Only registered voters of the county shall be eligible to hold the office of council member.

(c) **Election and Terms.** The regular election of council members shall be held on the _____ of _____ in each odd- [even-] numbered year, in the manner provided by law. At the first election under this charter _____ council members shall be elected; the _____ [one-half plus one] candidates receiving the greatest number of votes shall serve for terms of four years, and the _____ [remainder of the council] candidates receiving the next greatest number of votes shall serve for terms of two years. Commencing at the next regular election and at all subsequent elections, all council members shall be elected for four-year terms. The terms of council members shall begin the _____ day of _____ after their election.

NOTE: If staggered terms are not desired, use the following section:
[(c) **Election and Terms.** The regular election of council members shall be held on the _____ day of _____ every _____ years beginning in _____. The terms of council members shall be _____ years beginning the _____ day of _____ after their election.]

Alternative II: Election at Large with District Residency Requirement

(a) Composition. There shall be a county council of [odd-number] members; not more than one shall reside in each of the [odd-number] districts provided for in Article VI. All shall be nominated and elected by the voters of the county at large.

(b) Eligibility. Only registered voters of the county shall be eligible to hold the office of council member.

(c) Election and Terms. The regular election of council members shall be held on the _____ of _____ in each odd- [even-] numbered year, in the manner provided by law. At the first election under this charter _____ council members shall be elected; the _____ candidates receiving the greatest number of votes shall serve for terms of four years, and the _____ candidates receiving the next greatest number of votes shall serve for terms of two years. Thereafter, all council members shall be elected for four-year terms. The terms of council members shall begin the _____ day of _____ after their election.

NOTE: If staggered terms are not desired, use the following section.
[(c) **Election and Terms.** The regular election of council members shall be held on the _____ day of _____ every _____ years beginning in _____. The terms of council members shall be _____ years beginning the _____ day of _____ after their election.]

Alternative III: Mixed At-Large and Single-Member District System

(a) Composition. There shall be a county council of [odd-number] members. _____ shall be nominated and elected by the voters of the county at large, and _____ shall be nominated and elected by the voters of each of the _____ council districts, as provided in Article VI.

(b) Eligibility. Only registered voters of the county shall be eligible to hold the office of council member.

(c) Election and Terms. The terms of council members shall be _____ years beginning the _____ day of _____ after their election.

Alternative IV: Single-Member District System

(a) **Composition.** There shall be a county council composed of [odd-number] members. One council member shall be nominated and elected by the voters in each of [odd-number] council districts, as provided in Article VI.

(b) **Eligibility.** Only registered voters of the county shall be eligible to hold the office of council member.

(c) **Election and Terms.** The regular election of council members shall be held on the _____ of _____ in each odd- [even-] numbered year, in the manner provided by law. At the first election under this charter _____ council members shall be elected; council members from odd-numbered districts shall serve for terms of two years, and council members from even-numbered districts shall serve for terms of four years. Thereafter, all council members shall serve for terms of four years. The terms of council members shall begin the _____ day of _____ after their election.

NOTE: If staggered terms are not desired, use the following section.
[(c) **Election and Terms.** The regular election of council members shall be held on the _____ day of _____ every _____ years beginning in _____. The terms of council members shall be _____ years beginning the _____ day of _____ after their election.]

Alternative V (Proportional Representation)

(a) **Composition and Terms.** There shall be a county council of [odd-number] members elected by the registered voters of the county at large for a term of _____ years.

(b) **Eligibility.** Only registered voters of the county shall be eligible to hold the office of council member.

(c) **Election.** The regular election of council members shall be held on the _____ of _____ in each odd- [even-] numbered year. The council shall be elected by proportional representation by the method of the single transferable vote.

Section 2.03. Chairman of the Council.

Alternative I

The county council shall elect from among its members officers of the county who shall have the titles of chairman and vice chairman of the council, each of whom shall serve at the pleasure of the council. The chairman shall preside at meetings of the council, represent the county in intergovernmental relationships, appoint with the advice and consent of the council the members of citizen advisory boards and commissions, present an annual state of the county message, and perform other duties specified by the council. The chairman shall be recognized as head of the county government for all ceremonial purposes and by the governor for purposes of military law but shall have no administrative duties. The vice chairman shall act as chairman during the absence or disability of the chairman.

Alternative II

NOTE: If Alternative II is used, Section 2.02(a) should be modified to read as follows: "There shall be a county council composed of the chairman of the council and [even-number] council members elected as provided in Section 2.02(c); the chairman shall be elected as provided in Section 2.03." Section 2.02(c) should be modified to provide for election of an even number of council members by whichever method is used.

At each regular election a Chairman of the Council shall be elected for a term of _____ [the same term as other council members] years. The chairman shall be a member of the county council and shall preside at meetings of the council, represent the county in intergovernmental relationships, appoint with the advice and consent of the council the members of citizen advisory boards and commissions, present an annual state of the county message, and perform other duties specified by the council. The chairman shall be recognized as head of the county government for all ceremonial purposes and by the governor for purposes of military law but shall have no administrative duties. The council shall elect from its members a vice chairman who shall act as chairman during the absence or disability of the chairman and, if a vacancy occurs, shall become chairman for the remainder of the unexpired term.

Section 2.04. Compensation; Expenses.

The county council may determine the annual salary of the council members by ordinance, but no ordinance increasing such salary shall become effective until the date of commencement of the terms of council members elected at the next regular election. The council members shall receive their actual and necessary expenses incurred in the performance of their duties of office.

Section 2.05. Prohibitions.

(a) **Holding Other Office.** Except where authorized by law, no council member shall hold any other elected public office during the term for which the member was elected to the council. No council member shall hold any other county office or employment during the terms for which the member was elected to the council. No former council member shall hold any compensated appointive office or employment with the county until one year after the expiration of the term for which the member was elected to the council. Nothing in this section shall be construed to prohibit the council from selecting any current or former council member to represent the county on the governing board of any regional or other intergovernmental agency.

(b) **Appointments and Removals.** Neither the county council nor any of its members shall in any manner control or demand the appointment or removal of any county administrative officer or employee whom the county manager or any subordinate of the county manager is empowered to appoint, but the council may express its views and fully and freely discuss with the county manager anything pertaining to appointment and removal of such officers and employees.

(c) **Interference with Administration.** Except for the purpose of inquiries and investigations under §2.09, the council or its members shall deal with county officers and employees who are subject to the direction and supervision of the county manager solely through the county manager, and neither the council nor its member shall give orders to any such officer or employee, either publicly or privately.

Section 2.06. Vacancies; Forfeiture of Office; Filling of Vacancies.

(a) **Vacancies.** The office of a council member shall become vacant upon the member's death, resignation, removal from office or forfeiture of office in any manner authorized by law.

(b) **Forfeiture of Office.** A council member shall forfeit that office if the council member

(1)   lacks at any time during the term of office for which elected any qualification for the office prescribed by this charter or by law,

(2)   violates any express prohibition of this charter,

(3)   is convicted of a crime involving moral turpitude, or

(4)   fails to attend three consecutive regular meetings of the council without beingexcused by the council.

(c) **Filling of Vacancies.** A vacancy in the county council shall be filled for the remainder of the unexpired term, if any, at the next regular election following not less than 60 days upon the occurrence of the vacancy, but the council by a majority vote of all its remaining members shall appoint a qualified person to fill the vacancy until the person elected to serve the remainder of the unexpired term takes office. If the council fails to do so within 30 days following the occurrence of the vacancy, the election authorities shall call a special election to fill the vacancy, to be held not sooner than 90 days and not later than 120 days following the occurrence of the vacancy, and to be otherwise governed by law. Notwithstanding the requirement in §2.11, if at any time the membership of the council is reduced to less than _____, the remaining members may by majority action appoint additional members to raise the membership to _____.

Section 2.07. Judge of Qualifications.

The county council shall be the judge of the election and qualifications of its members and of the grounds for forfeiture of their office. The council shall have the power to set additional standards of conduct for its members beyond those specified in the charter and may provide for such penalties as it deems appropriate, including forfeiture of office. In order to exercise these powers, the council shall have power to subpoena witnesses, administer oaths and require the production of evidence. A member charged with conduct constituting grounds for forfeiture of office shall be entitled to a public hearing on demand, and notice of such hearing shall be published in one or more newspapers of general circulation in the county at least one week in advance of the hearing. Decisions made by the council under this section shall be subject to judicial review.

Section 2.08. County Clerk.

The county council shall appoint an officer of the county who shall have the title of county clerk. The county clerk shall give notice of council meetings to its members and the public, keep the journal of its proceedings and perform such other duties as are assigned by this charter or by the council or by state law.

Section 2.09. Investigations.

The county council may make investigations into the affairs of the county and the conduct of any county department, office or agency and for this purpose may subpoena witnesses, administer oaths, take testimony and require the production of evidence. Failure or refusal to obey a lawful order issued in the exercise of these powers by the council shall be a misdemeanor punishable by a fine of not more than $_____, or by imprisonment for not more than _____, or both.

Section 2.10. Independent Audit.

The county council shall provide for an independent annual audit of all county accounts and may provide for more frequent audits as it deems necessary. Such audits shall be made by a certified public accountant or firm of such accountants who have no personal interest, direct or indirect, in the fiscal affairs of the county government or any of its officers. The council may, without requiring competitive bids, designate such accountant or firm annually or for a period not exceeding three years, but the designation for any particular fiscal year shall be made no later than 30 days after the beginning of such fiscal year. If the state makes such an audit, the council may accept it as satisfying the requirements of this section.

Section 2.11. Procedure.

(a) Meetings. The council shall meet regularly at least once in every month at such times and places as the council may prescribe by rule. Special meetings may be held on the call of the chairman or of _____ or more members and, whenever practicable, upon no less than twelve hours notice to each member. Except as allowed by state law, all meetings shall be public; however, the council may recess for the purpose of discussing in a closed or executive session limited to its own membership any matter which would tend to defame or prejudice the character or reputation of any person, if the general subject matter for consideration is expressed in the motion calling for such session and final action on such motion is not taken by the council until the matter is placed on the agenda.

(b) Rules and Journal. The county council shall determine its own rules and order of business and shall provide for keeping a journal of its proceedings. This journal shall be a public record.

(c) Voting. Voting, except on procedural motions, shall be by roll call and the ayes and nays shall be recorded in the journal. _____ members of the council shall constitute a quorum, but a smaller number may adjourn from time to time and may compel the attendance of absent members in the manner and subject to the penalties prescribed by the rules of the council. No action of the council, except as otherwise provided in the preceding sentence and in §2.06, shall be valid or binding unless adopted by the affirmative vote of _____ or more members of the council.

Section 2.12. Action Requiring an Ordinance.

In addition to other acts required by law or by specific provision of this charter to be done by ordinance, those acts of the county council shall be by ordinance which:

   (1) Adopt or amend an administrative code or establish, alter, or abolish any county department, office or agency;

   (2) Provide for a fine or other penalty or establish a rule or regulation for violation of which a fine or other penalty is imposed;

   (3) Levy taxes;

   (4) Grant, renew or extend a franchise;

   (5) Regulate the rate charged for its service by a public utility;

   (6) Authorize the borrowing of money;

   (7) Convey or lease or authorize the conveyance or lease of any lands of the county;

   (8) Regulate land use and development; and

   (9) Amend or repeal any ordinance previously adopted.

Acts other than those referred to in the preceding sentence may be done either by ordinance or by resolution.

Section 2.13. Ordinances in General.

(a) Forum. Every proposed ordinance shall be introduced in writing and in the form required for final adoption. No ordinance shall contain more than one subject which shall be clearly expressed in its title. The enacting clause shall be "The county of _____ hereby ordains ..." Any ordinance which repeals or amends an existing ordinance or part of the county code shall set out in full the ordinance, sections or subsections to be repealed or amended, and shall indicate matters to be omitted by enclosing it in brackets or by strikeout type and shall indicate new matters by underscoring or by italics.

(b) Procedure. An ordinance may be introduced by any member at any regular or special meeting of the council. Upon introduction of any ordinance, the county clerk shall distribute a copy to each council member and to the county manager, shall file a reasonable number of copies in the office of the county clerk and such other public places as the council may designate, and shall publish the ordinance together with a notice setting out the time and place for a public hearing thereon and for its consideration by the council. The public hearing shall follow the publication by at least seven days, may be held separately or in connection with a regular or special council meeting and may be adjourned from time to time; all persons interested shall have an opportunity to be heard. After the hearing the council may adopt the ordinance with or without amendment or reject it, but if it is amended as to any matter of substance, the council may not adopt it until the ordinance or its amended sections have been subjected to all the procedures herein before required in the case of a newly introduced ordinance. As soon as practicable after adoption, the clerk shall have the ordinance and a notice of its adoption published and available at a reasonable price.

(c) Effective Date. Except as otherwise provided in this charter, every adopted ordinance shall become effective at the expiration of 30 days after adoption or at any later date specified therein.

(d) "Publish" Defined. As used in this section, the term "publish" means to print in one or more newspapers of general circulation in the county: (1) The ordinance or a brief summary thereof, and (2) the places where copies of it have been filed and the times when they are available for public inspection and purchase at a reasonable price.

Section 2.14. Emergency Ordinances.

To meet a public emergency affecting life, health, property or the public peace, the county council may adopt one or more emergency ordinances, but such ordinances may not levy taxes, grant, renew or extend a franchise, regulate the rate charged by any public utility for its services or authorize the borrowing of money except as provided in §5.07(b). An emergency ordinance shall be introduced in the form and manner prescribed for ordinances generally, except that it shall be plainly designated as an emergency ordinance and shall contain, after the enacting clause, a declaration stating that an emergency exists and describing it in clear and specific terms. An emergency ordinance may be adopted with or without amendment or rejected at the meeting at which it is introduced, but the affirmative vote of at least _____ members shall be required for adoption. After its adoption the ordinance shall be published and printed as prescribed for other adopted ordinances. It shall become effective upon adoption or at such later time as it may specify. Every emergency ordinance except one made pursuant to §5.07(b) shall automatically stand repealed as of the 61st day following the date on which it was adopted, but this shall not prevent reenactment of the ordinance in the manner specified in this section if the emergency still exists. An emergency ordinance may also be repealed by adoption of a repealing ordinance in the same manner specified in this section for adoption of emergency ordinances.

Section 2.15. Codes of Technical Regulations.

The county council may adopt any standard code of technical regulations by reference thereto in an adopting ordinance. The procedure and requirements governing such an adopting ordinance shall be as prescribed for ordinances generally except that:

(1)   The requirements of §2.13 for distribution and filing of copies of the ordinance shall be construed to include copies of the code of technical regulations as well as of the adopting ordinance, and

(2)   A copy of each adopted code of technical regulations as well as of the adopting ordinance shall be authenticated and recorded by the county clerk pursuant to §2.16(a).

Copies of any adopted code of technical regulations shall be made available by the county clerk for distribution or for purchase at a reasonable price.

Section 2.16. Authentication and Recording; Codification; Printing.

(a) Authentication and Recording. The county clerk shall authenticate by signing and shall record in full in a properly indexed book kept for the purpose all ordinances and resolutions adopted by the county council.

(b) Codification. Within three years after adoption of this charter and at least every ten years thereafter, the county council shall provide for the preparation of a general codification of all county ordinances and resolutions having the force and effect of law. The general codification shall be adopted by the council by ordinance and shall be published promptly in bound or loose-leaf form, together with this charter and any amendments thereto, pertinent provisions of the constitution and other laws of the state of _____, and such codes of technical regulations and other rules and regulations as the council may specify. This compilation shall be known and cited officially as the _____ county code. Copies of the code shall be furnished to county officers, placed in libraries and public offices for free public reference and made available for purchase by the public at a reasonable price fixed by the council.

(c) Printing of Ordinances and Resolutions. The county council shall cause each ordinance and resolution having the force and effect of law and each amendment to this charter to be printed promptly following its adoption, and the printed ordinances, resolutions and charter amendments shall be distributed or sold to the public at reasonable prices as fixed by the council. Following publication of the first _____ County Code and at all times thereafter, the ordinances, resolutions and charter amendments shall be printed in substantially the same style as the code currently in effect and shall be suitable in form for integration therein. The council shall make such further arrangements as it deems desirable with respect to reproduction and distribution of any current changes in or additions to the provisions of the constitution and other laws of the state of _____, or the codes of technical regulations and other rules and regulations included in the code.

Article III
COUNTY MANAGER

Section 3.01. Appointment; Qualifications; Compensation.

The county council by a majority vote of its total membership shall appoint a county manager for an indefinite term and fix the manager's compensation. The county manager shall be appointed solely on the basis of executive and administrative qualifications. The manager need not be a resident of the county or state at the time of appointment, but may reside outside the county while in office only with the approval of the council.

Section 3.02. Removal.

The county manager may be suspended by a resolution approved by the majority of the total membership of the county council which shall set forth the reasons for suspension and proposed removal. A copy of such resolution shall be served immediately upon the county manager. The county manager shall have fifteen days in which to reply thereto in writing, and upon request, shall be afforded a public hearing, which shall occur not earlier than ten days nor later than fifteen days after such hearing is requested. After the public hearing, if one is requested, and after full consideration, the county council by a majority vote of its total membership may adopt a final resolution of removal. The county manager shall continue to receive full salary until the effective date of a final resolution of removal.

Section 3.03. Acting County Manager.

By letter filed with the county clerk, the county manager shall designate a county officer or employee to exercise the powers and perform the duties of county manager during the manager's temporary absence or disability. The county council may revoke such designation at any time and appoint another officer of the county to serve until the county manager returns.

Section 3.04. Powers and Duties of the County Manager.

The county manager shall be the chief administrative officer of the county, responsible to the Council for the administration of all county affairs placed in the manager's charge by or under this charter. The county manager shall:

(1) Appoint and, when necessary for the good of the service, suspend or remove all county employees and appointive administrative officers provided for by or under this charter, except as otherwise provided by law, this charter or personnel rules adopted pursuant to this charter. The county manager may authorize any administrative officer subject to the manager's direction and supervision to exercise these powers with respect to subordinates in that officer's department, office or agency;

(2) Direct and supervise the administration of all departments, offices and agencies of the county, except as otherwise provided by this charter or by law;

(3) Attend all county council meetings. The county manager shall have the right to take part in discussion but shall not vote;

(4) See that all laws, provisions of this charter and acts of the county council, subject to enforcement by the county manager or by officers subject to the manager's direction and supervision, are faithfully executed;

(5) Prepare and submit the annual budget and capital program to the county council;

(6) Submit to the county council and make available to the public a complete report on the finances and administrative activities of the county as of the end of each fiscal year;

(7) Make such other reports as the county council may require concerning the operations of county departments, offices and agencies subject to the county manager's direction and supervision;

(8) Keep the county council fully advised as to the financial condition and future needs of the county;

(9) Make recommendations to the county council concerning the affairs of the county;

(10) Provide staff support services for the council members; and

(11) Perform such other duties as are specified in this charter or may be required by the county council.

Article IV
DEPARTMENTS, OFFICES AND AGENCIES

Section 4.01. General Provisions.

(a) **Creation of Departments.** The county council may establish county departments, offices or agencies in addition to those created by this charter and may prescribe the functions of all departments, offices and agencies, except that no function assigned by this charter to a particular department, office or agency may be discontinued or, unless this charter specifically so provides, assigned to any other.

(b) **Direction by County Manager.** All departments, offices and agencies under the direction and supervision of the county manager shall be administered by an officer appointed by and subject to the direction and supervision of the manager. With the consent of council, the county manager may serve as the head of one or more such departments, offices or agencies or may appoint one person as the head of two or more of them.

Section 4.02. Personnel System.

(a) **Merit Principle.**

All appointments and promotions of county officers and employees shall be made solely on the basis of merit and fitness demonstrated by a valid and reliable examination or other evidence of competence.

(b) **Merit System.** Consistent with all applicable federal and state laws the county council shall provide by ordinance for the establishment, regulation and maintenance of a merit system governing personnel policies necessary to effective administration of the employees of the county's departments, offices and agencies, including but not limited to classification and pay plans, examinations, force reduction, removals, working conditions, provisional and exempt appointments, in-service training, grievances and relationships with employee organizations.

Section 4.03. Legal Officer.

Alternative I

There shall be a legal officer of the county appointed by the county manager as provided in §4.01(b). The legal officer shall serve as chief legal adviser to the county council, the manager and all county department, offices and agencies, shall represent the county in all legal proceedings and shall perform any other duties prescribed by state law, by this charter or by ordinance.

Alternative II

There shall be a legal officer of the county appointed by the county manager subject to confirmation by the county council. The legal officer shall serve as the chief legal adviser to the council, the manager and all county departments, offices and agencies, shall represent the county in all legal proceedings and shall perform any other duties prescribed by state law, by this charter or by ordinance.

Alternative III

There shall be a legal officer of the county appointed by the county council. The legal officer shall serve as chief legal adviser to the council, the county manager and all county departments, offices and agencies, shall represent the county in all legal proceedings and shall perform any other duties prescribed by state law, by this charter or by ordinance.

Section 4.04. Planning.

Consistent with all applicable federal and state laws with respect to land use, development and environmental protection, the county council shall:

(1) Designate an agency or agencies to carry out the planning function and such decision-making responsibilities as may be specified by ordinance;

(2) Adopt a comprehensive plan and determine to what extent zoning and other land use control ordinances must be consistent with the plan; and

(3) Adopt development regulations, to be specified by ordinance, to implement the plan.

Article V
FINANCIAL PROCEDURES

Section 5.01. Fiscal Year.

The fiscal year of the county shall begin on the first day of _____ and end on the last day of _____ .

Section 5.02. Submission of Budget and Budget Message.

On or before the _____ day of _____ of each year, the county manager shall submit to the county council a budget for the ensuing fiscal year and an accompanying message.

Section 5.03. Budget Message.

The county manager's message shall explain the budget both in fiscal terms and in terms of the work programs. It shall outline the proposed financial policies of the county for the ensuing fiscal year, describe the important features of the budget, indicate any major changes from the current year in financial policies, expenditures, and revenues together with the reasons for such changes, summarize the county's debt position and include such other material as the county manager deems desirable.

Section 5.04. Budget.

The budget shall provide a complete financial plan of all county funds and activities for the ensuing fiscal year and, except as required by law or this charter, shall be in such form as the county manager deems desirable or the county council may require. The budget shall begin with a clear general summary of its contents; shall show in detail all estimated income, indicating the proposed property tax levy, and all proposed expenditures, including debt service, for the ensuing fiscal year; and shall be so arranged as to show comparative figures for actual and estimated income and expenditures of the current fiscal year and actual income and expenditures of the preceding fiscal year. It shall indicate in separate sections:

(1)   The proposed goals and objectives and expenditures for current operations during the ensuing fiscal year, detailed for each fund by organization unit, and program, purpose or activity, and the method of financing such expenditures;

(2)   Proposed capital expenditures during the ensuing fiscal year, detailed for each fund by organization unit when practicable, and the proposed method of financing each such capital expenditure; and

(3)   The anticipated income and expense and profit and loss for the ensuing year for each utility or other enterprise fund operated by the county.

For any fund, the total of proposed expenditures shall not exceed the total of estimated income plus carried forward fund balance, exclusive of reserves.

Section 5.05. County Council Action on Budget.

(a) Notice and Hearing. The county council shall publish in one or more newspapers of general circulation in the county the general summary of the budget and a notice stating:

(1)   The times and places where copies of the message and budget are available for inspection by the public, and

(2)   The time and place, not less than two weeks after such publication, for a public hearing on the budget.

(b) Amendment Before Adoption. After the public hearing, the county council may adopt the budget with or without amendment. In amending the budget, it may add or increase programs or amounts and may delete or decrease any programs or amounts, except expenditures required by law or for debt service or for an estimated cash deficit, provided that no amendment to the budget shall increase the authorized expenditures to an amount greater than total estimated income.

(c) Adoption. The county council shall adopt the budget on or before the _____ day of the _____ month of the fiscal year currently ending. If it fails to adopt the budget by this date, the budget proposed by the county manager shall go into effect.

Section 5.06 Appropriation and Revenue Ordinances.

To implement the adopted budget, the county council shall adopt, prior to the beginning of the fiscal year:

(a) an appropriation ordinance making appropriations by department or major organizational unit and authorizing a single appropriation for each program or activity;

(b) a tax levy ordinance authorizing the property tax levy or levies and setting the tax rate or rates; and

(c) any other ordinances required to authorize new revenues or to amend the rates or other features of existing taxes or other revenue sources.

Section 5.07. Amendments after Adoption.

(a) **Supplemental Appropriations.** If during the fiscal year the county manager certifies that there are available for appropriation revenues in excess of those estimated in the budget, the county council by ordinance may make supplemental appropriations for the year up to the amount of such excess.

(b) **Emergency Appropriations.** To meet a public emergency affecting life, health, property or the public peace, the county council may make emergency appropriations. Such appropriations may be made by emergency ordinance in accordance with the provisions of §2.14. To the extent that there are no available unappropriated revenues or a sufficient fund balance to meet such appropriations, the council may by such emergency ordinance authorize the issuance of emergency notes, which may be renewed from time to time, but the emergency notes and renewals of any fiscal year shall be paid not later than the last day of the fiscal year next succeeding that in which the emergency appropriation was made.

(c) **Reduction of Appropriations.** If at any time during the fiscal year it appears probable to the county manager that the revenues or fund balances available will be insufficient to finance the expenditures for which appropriations have been authorized, the manager shall report to the county council without delay, indicating the estimated amount of the deficit, any remedial action taken by the manager and recommendations as to any other steps to be taken. The council shall then take such further action as it deems necessary to prevent or reduce any deficit and for that purpose it may by ordinance reduce one or more appropriations.

(d) **Transfer of Appropriations.** At any time during the fiscal year the county council may by resolution transfer part or all of the unencumbered appropriation balance from one department or major organizational unit to the appropriation for other departments or major organizational units. The manager may transfer part or all of any unencumbered appropriation balances among programs within a department or organizational unit and shall report such transfers to the council in writing in a timely manner.

(e) **Limitation; Effective Date.** No appropriation for debt service may be reduced or transferred, and no appropriation may be reduced below any amount required by law to be appropriated or by more than the amount of the unencumbered balance thereof. The supplemental and emergency appropriations and reduction or transfer of appropriations authorized by this section may be made effective immediately upon adoption.

Section 5.08. Lapse of Appropriations.

Every appropriation, except an appropriation for a capital expenditure, shall lapse at the close of the fiscal year to the extent that it has not been expended or encumbered. An appropriation for a capital expenditure shall continue in force until expended, revised or repealed; the purpose of any such appropriation shall be deemed abandoned if three years pass without any disbursement from or encumbrance of the appropriation.

Section 5.09. Administration of the Budget.

The county council shall provide by ordinance the procedures for administering the budget.

Section 5.10. Overspending of Appropriations Prohibited.

No payment shall be made or obligation incurred against any allotment or appropriation except in accordance with appropriations duly made and unless the county manager or the manager's designee first certifies that there is a sufficient unencumbered balance in such allotment or appropriation and that sufficient funds therefrom are or will be available to cover the claim or meet the obligation when it becomes due and payable. Any authorization of payment or incurring of obligation in violation of the provisions of this charter shall be void and any payment so made illegal. A violation of this provision shall be cause for removal of any officer who knowingly authorized or made such payment or incurred such obligation. Such officer may also be liable to the county for any amount so paid. Except where prohibited by law, however, nothing in this charter shall be construed to prevent the making or authorizing of payments or making of contracts for capital improvements to be financed wholly or partly by the issuance of bonds or to prevent the making of any contract or lease providing for payments beyond the end of the fiscal year, but only if such action is made or approved by ordinance.

Section 5.11. Capital Program.

(a) Submission to County Council. The county manager shall prepare and submit to the county council a five- [six-] year capital program no later than three months prior to the final date for submission of the budget.

(b) Contents. The capital program shall include:
   (1) A clear general summary of its contents;
   (2) A list of all capital improvements and other capital expenditures which are proposed to be undertaken during the five [six] fiscal years next ensuing, with appropriate supporting information as to the necessity for each;
   (3) Cost estimates and recommended time schedules for each improvement or other capital expenditure;
   (4) Method of financing upon which each capital expenditure is to be reliant; and
   (5) The estimated annual cost of operating and maintaining the facilities to be constructed or acquired.

The above shall be revised and extended each year with regard to capital improvements still pending or in process of construction or acquisition.

Section 5.12. County Council Action on Capital Program.

(a) Notice and Hearing. The county council shall publish in one or more newspapers of general circulation in the county the general summary of the capital program and a notice stating:
   (1) The times and places where copies of the capital program are available for inspection by the public, and
   (2) The time and place, not less than two weeks after such publication, for a public hearing on the capital program.

(b) Adoption. The county council by resolution shall adopt the capital program with or without amendment after the public hearing and on or before the _____ day of the _____ month of the current fiscal year.

Section 5.13. Public Records.

Copies of the budget, capital program and appropriation and revenue ordinances shall be public records and shall be made available to the public at suitable places in the county.

Article VI
COUNTY ELECTIONS

Section 6.01. County Elections.

(a) Regular Elections. The regular county elections shall be held at the time established by state law.

(b) Registered Voter Defined. All citizens legally registered under the constitution and laws of the state of _____ to vote in the county shall be registered voters of the county within the meaning of this charter.

(c) Conduct of Elections. The provisions of the general election laws of the state of _____ shall apply to elections held under this charter. All elections provided for by the charter shall be conducted by the election authorities established by law. For the conduct of county elections, for the prevention of fraud in such elections and for the recount of ballots in cases of doubt or fraud, the county council shall adopt ordinances consistent with law and this charter, and the election authorities may adopt further regulations consistent with law and this charter and the ordinances of the council. Such ordinances and regulations pertaining to elections shall be publicized in the manner of county ordinances generally.

Section 6.02. Council Districts; Adjustment of Districts (for use with **Alternatives II, III and IV of §2.01**)

(a) **Number of Districts.** There shall be _____ county council districts.

(b) **Districting Commission; Composition; Appointment; Terms; Vacancies; Compensation.**

(1) There shall be a districting commission consisting of five members. No more than two commission members may belong to the same political party. The county council shall appoint four members. These four members shall, with the affirmative vote of at least three, choose the fifth member who shall be the chairman.

(2) No member of the commission shall be employed by the county or any political sub- division of the county, or hold any other elected or appointed position in the county or any political subdivision of the county.

(3) The county council shall appoint the commission no later than one year and five months before the first general election of the county council after each federal decennial census. The commission's term shall end upon adoption of a districting plan, as set forth in §6.02(c).

(4) In the event of a vacancy on the Commission by death, resignation or otherwise, the county council shall appoint a new member enrolled in the same political party from which his or her predecessor was selected, to serve the balance of the term remaining.

(5) No member of the districting commission shall be removed from office by the county council except for cause and upon notice and hearing.

(6) The members of the commission shall serve without compensation except that each member shall be allowed actual and necessary expenses to be audited in the same manner as other county charges.

(7) The commission may hire or contract for necessary staff assistance and may require agencies of county government to provide technical assistance. The commission shall have a budget as provided by the county council.

(c) **Powers and Duties of the Commission; Hearings, Submissions and Approval of Plan.**

(1) Following each decennial census, the commission shall consult the county council and shall prepare a plan for dividing the county into districts for the election of council members. In preparing the plan, the commission shall be guided by the criteria set forth in §6.02(d). The report on the plan shall include a map and description of districts recommended.

(2) The commission shall hold one or more public hearings not less than one month before it submits the plan to the county council. The commission shall make its plan available to the public for inspection and comment not less than one month before its public hearing.

(3) The commission shall submit its plan to the county council not less than one year before the first general election of the county council after each decennial census.

(4) The plan shall be deemed adopted by the county council unless disapproved within three weeks by the vote of the majority of all members of the county council. If the county council fails to adopt the plan, it shall return the plan to the commission with its objections, and with the objections of individual members of the council.

(5) Upon rejection of its plan, the commission shall prepare a revised plan and shall submit such revised plan to the county council no later than nine months before the first general election of the county council after the decennial census. Such revised plan shall be deemed adopted by the county council unless disapproved within two weeks by the vote of two-thirds of all of the members of the county council and unless, by a vote of two-thirds of all of its members, the county council votes to file a petition in the _____ Court, _____ County, for a determination that the plan fails to meet the requirements of this charter. The county council shall file its petition no later than ten days after its disapproval of the plan. Upon a final determination upon appeal, if any, that the plan meets the requirements of this charter, the plan shall be deemed adopted by the county council and the commission shall deliver the plan to the county clerk. The plan delivered to the county clerk shall include a map and description of the districts.

(6) If in any year population figures are not available at least one year and five months before the first general election following the decennial census, the county council may by ordinance shorten the time periods provided for districting commission action in subsections (2), (3), (4), and (5) of this section.

(d) **Districting Plan; Criteria.** In preparation of its plan for dividing the county into districts for the election of council members, the commission shall apply the following criteria which, to the extent practicable, shall be applied and given priority in the order in which they are herein set forth.

(1) Districts shall be equal in population except where deviations from equality result from the application of the provisions hereinafter set forth, but no such deviation may exceed five percent of the average population for all county council districts according to the figures available from the most recent census.

(2) Districts shall consist of contiguous territory; but land areas separated by waterways shall not be included in the same district unless said waterways are traversed by highway bridges, tunnels or regularly scheduled ferry services both termini of which are within the district, except that, population permitting, islands not connected to the mainland or to other islands by bridge, tunnel or regular ferry services shall be included in the same district as the nearest land area within the county and, where such subdivisions exist, within the same ward or equivalent subdivision as described in subsection (5), below.

(3) No city block shall be divided in the formation of districts.

(4) A municipality within a county shall be divided among as few districts as possible.

(5) In the establishment of districts within counties whose territory is divided into wards or equivalent subdivisions whose boundaries have remained substantially unaltered for at least fifteen years, the number of such wards or equivalent subdivisions whose territory is divided among more than one district shall be as small as possible.

(6) Consistent with the foregoing provisions, the aggregate length of all district boundaries shall be as short as possible.

(e) **Effect of Enactment.** The new county council districts and boundaries as of the date of enactment shall supersede previous council districts and boundaries for all purposes of the next regular county election, including nominations. The new districts and boundaries shall supersede previous districts and boundaries for all other purposes as of the date on which all council members elected at that regular county election take office.

[**Section 6.03. Initiative and Referendum.**

The powers of initiative and referendum are hereby reserved to the electors of the county. The provisions of the election law of the state of _____, as they currently exist or may hereafter be amended or superseded, shall govern the exercise of the powers of initiative and referendum under this charter.]

NOTE: Section 6.03 is in brackets because not all states provide for the initiative and referendum and it is possible that not all counties within the states that do provide for it will choose to include the option in their charters.

Article VII
GENERAL PROVISIONS

Section 7.01. Conflicts of Interest; Board of Ethics.

(a) Conflicts of Interest. The use of public office for private gain is prohibited. The county council shall implement this prohibition by ordinance. Regulations to this end shall include but not be limited to: acting in an official capacity on matters in which the official has a private financial interest clearly separate from that of the general public; the acceptance of gifts and other things of value; acting in a private capacity on matters dealt with as a public official, the use of confidential information; and appearances by county officials before other county agencies on behalf of private interests. This ordinance shall provide for reasonable public disclosure of finances by officials with major decision-making authority over monetary expenditures and contractual matters and, insofar as permissible under state law, shall provide for fines and imprisonment for violations.

(b) Board of Ethics. The county council shall, by ordinance, establish an independent board of ethics to administer and enforce the conflict of interest and financial disclosure ordinances. No member of the board may hold elective or appointive office under the county or any other government or hold any political party office. Insofar as possible under state law, the county council shall authorize the board to issue binding advisory opinions, conduct investigations on its own initiative and on referral or complaint, refer cases for prosecution, impose administrative fines, and to hire independent counsel. The county council shall appropriate sufficient funds to the board of ethics to enable it to perform the duties assigned to it.

Section 7.02. Prohibitions.

(a) Activities Prohibited.

(1)   No person shall be appointed to or removed from, or in any way favored or discriminated against with respect to any county position or appointive county administrative office because of race, gender, age, handicap, religion, country of origin or political affiliation.

(2)   No person shall willfully make any false statement, certificate, mark, rating or report in regard to any test, certification or appointment under the provisions of this charter or the rules and regulations made thereunder, or in any manner commit or attempt to commit any fraud preventing the impartial execution of such provisions, rules and regulations.

(3)   No person who seeks appointment or promotion with respect to any county position or appointive county administrative office shall directly or indirectly give, render or pay any money, service or other valuable thing to any person for or in connection with his or her test, appointment, proposed appointment, promotion or proposed promotion.

(4)   No person shall knowingly or willfully solicit or assist in soliciting any assessment, subscription or contribution for any political party or political purpose to be used in conjunction with any county election from any county employee.

(5)　No county employee shall knowingly or willfully make, solicit or receive any contribution to the campaign funds of any political party or committee to be used in a county election or to campaign funds to be used in support of or in opposition to any candidate for election to county office or county ballot issue. Further, no county employee shall knowingly or willfully participate in any aspect of any political campaign on behalf of or in opposition to any candidate for county office. This section shall not be construed to limit any person's right to exercise rights as a citizen to express opinions or to cast a vote nor shall it be construed to prohibit any person from active participation in political campaigns at any other level of government.

(b) Penalties. Any person convicted of a violation of this section shall be ineligible for a period of five years following such conviction to hold any county office or position and, if an officer or employee of the county, shall immediately forfeit his or her office or position. The county council shall establish by ordinance such further penalties as it may deem appropriate.

Article VIII
CHARTER AMENDMENT

Section 8.01. Proposal of Amendment.

Amendments to this charter may be framed and proposed:

(a) In the manner provided by law, or

(b) By ordinance of the county council containing the full text of the proposed amendment and effective upon adoption, or

(c) By report of a charter commission created by ordinance; or

(d) By the voters of the county.

When any five qualified voters initiate proceedings to amend the charter by filing with the county clerk an affidavit stating they will constitute the petitioners' committee and be responsible for circulating the petition and filing it in proper form, stating their names and addresses and specifying the address to which all notices to the committee are to be sent, and setting out in full the proposed charter amendment. Promptly after the affidavit of the petitioners' committee is filed the clerk shall issue the appropriate petition blanks to the petitioners' committee. The petitions shall contain or have attached thereto throughout their circulation the full text of the proposed charter amendment and must be signed by registered voters of the county in the number of at least twenty percent of the total number of registered voters at the last regular county election. The petitioners' committee may withdraw the petition at any time before the fifteenth day immediately preceding the day scheduled for the county vote on the amendment.

Section 8.02. Election.

Upon delivery to the county election authorities of the report of a charter commission or delivery by the county clerk of an adopted ordinance proposing an amendment pursuant to §8.01(b) or a petition finally determined sufficient proposing an amendment pursuant to §8.01(d), the election authorities shall submit the proposed amendment to the voters of the county at an election. Such election shall be announced by a notice containing the complete text of the proposed amendment and published in one or more newspapers of general circulation in the county at least 30 days prior to the date of the election. If the amendment is proposed by petition, the amendment may be withdrawn at any time prior to the fifteenth day preceding the day scheduled for the election by filing with the county clerk a request for withdrawal signed by at least four members of the petitioners' committee. The election shall be held not less than 60 and not more than 120 days after the adoption of the ordinance or report, or the final determination of sufficiency of the petition proposing the amendment. If no regular election is to be held within that period, the county council shall provide for a special election on the proposed amendment; otherwise, the holding of a special election shall be as specified in the state election law.

Section 8.03. Adoption of Amendment.

If a majority of the registered voters of the county voting upon a proposed charter amendment vote in favor of it, the amendment shall become effective at the time fixed in the amendment or, if no time is therein fixed, 30 days after its adoption by the voters.

Article IX
TRANSITION/SEPARABILITY PROVISIONS

Section 9.01. Officers and Employees.

(a) Rights and Privileges Preserved. Nothing in this charter except as otherwise specifically provided shall affect or impair the rights or privileges of persons who are county officers or employees at the time of its adoption.

(b) Continuance of Office or Employment. Except as specifically provided by this charter, if at the time this charter takes full effect a county administrative officer or employee holds any office or position which is or can be abolished by or under this charter, he or she shall continue in such office or position until the taking effect of some specific provision under this charter directing that he or she vacate the office or position.

(c) Personnel System. An employee holding a county position at the time this charter takes full effect, who was serving in that same or a comparable position at the time of its adoption, shall not be subject to competitive tests as a condition of continuance in the same position but in all other respects shall be subject to the personnel system provided for in §4.02.

Section 9.02. Departments, Offices and Agencies.

(a) Transfer of Powers. If a county department, office or agency is abolished by this charter, the powers and duties given it by law shall be transferred to the county department, office or agency designated in this charter or, if the charter makes no provision, designated by the county council.

(b) Property and Records. All property, records and equipment of any department, office or agency existing when this charter is adopted shall be transferred to the department, office or agency assuming its powers and duties, but, in the event that the powers or duties are to be discontinued or divided between units or in the event that any conflict arises regarding a transfer, such property, records or equipment shall be transferred to one or more departments, offices or agencies designated by the county council in accordance with this charter.

Section 9.03. Pending Matters.

All rights, claims, actions, orders, contracts and legal administrative proceedings shall continue except as modified pursuant to the provisions of this charter and in each case shall be maintained, carried on or dealt with by the county department, office or agency appropriate under this charter.

Section 9.04. Laws in Force.

(a) In General. All county ordinances, resolutions, orders and regulations which are in force when this charter becomes fully effective are repealed to the extent that they are inconsistent or interfere with the effective operation of this charter or of ordinances or resolutions adopted pursuant thereto. To the extent that the constitution and laws of the state of _____ permit, all laws relating to or affecting this county or its agencies, officers or employees which are in force when this charter becomes fully effective are superseded to the extent that they are inconsistent or interfere with the effective operation of this charter or of ordinances or resolutions adopted pursuant thereto.

(b) Specific Provisions. Without limitation of the general operation of subsection (a) or of the number or nature of the provisions to which it applies:

(1)   The following laws and parts of laws generally affecting counties or county agencies, officers or employees are inapplicable to the county of _____ or its agencies, officers or employees: [enumeration]

(2)   The following public local laws relating to the county of _____ are superseded: [enumeration]

(3)   The following ordinances, resolutions, orders and regulations of _____ [former county governing body] are repealed: [enumeration]

Section 9.05. Schedule.

(a) First Election. At the time of its adoption, this charter shall be in effect to the extent necessary in order that the first election of members of the county council may be conducted in accordance with the provisions of this charter. The first election shall be held on the _____ of _____. The _____ [county officials to be designated] shall prepared and adopt temporary regulations applicable only to the first election and designed to insure its proper conduct and to prevent fraud and provide for recount of ballots in cases of doubt or fraud.

(b) Time of Taking Full Effect. The charter shall be in full effect for all purposes on and after the date and time of the first meeting of the newly elected county council provided in §9.05(c).

(c) First Council Meeting. On the _____ of _____ following the first election of county council members under this charter, the newly elected members of the council shall meet at _____ [time] at [place]:

(1)   For the purpose of electing the [chairman and] vice chairman, appointing or considering the appointment of a county manager or acting county manager, and

choosing, if it so desires, one of its members to act as temporary clerk pending appointment of a county clerk pursuant to §2.08; and

NOTE: Omit bracketed words if Section 2.03, Alternative II is used.

(2) For the purpose of adopting ordinances and resolutions necessary to effect the transition of government under this charter and to maintain effective county government during that transition.

(d) Temporary Ordinances. In adopting ordinances as provided in §9.05(c), the county council shall follow the procedures prescribed in Article II, except that at its first meeting or any meeting held within 60 days thereafter, the council may adopt temporary ordinances to deal with cases in which there is an urgent need for prompt action in connection with the transition of government and in which the delay incident to the appropriate ordinance procedure would probably cause serious hardship or impairment of effective county government. Every temporary ordinance shall be plainly labelled as such but shall be introduced in the form and manner prescribed for ordinances generally. A temporary ordinance may be considered and may be adopted with or without amendment or rejected at the meeting at which it is introduced. After adoption of a temporary ordinance, the council shall cause it to be printed and published as prescribed for other adopted ordinances. A temporary ordinance shall become effective upon adoption or at such later time preceding automatic repeal under this subsection as it may specify[, and the referendum power shall not extend to any such ordinance]. Every temporary ordinance, including any amendments made thereto after adoption, shall automatically stand repealed as of the 91st day following the date on which it was adopted, renewed or otherwise continued except by adoption in the manner prescribed in Article II for ordinances of the kind concerned.

(e) Initial Expenses. The initial expenses of the county council, including the expense of recruiting a county manager, shall be paid by the county on vouchers signed by the council chairman.

(f) Initial Salary of Council Chairman and Council Members. The chairman of the council shall receive an annual salary in the amount of $_____ and each other council member in the amount of $_____, until such amount is changed by the council in accordance with the provisions of this charter.

Section 9.06. Separability.

If any provision of this charter is held invalid, the other provisions of the charter shall not be affected thereby. If the application of the charter or any of its provisions to any person or circumstance is held invalid, the application of the charter and its provisions to other persons or circumstances shall not be affected thereby.

— — — —

Editor's Note: A complete copy of this document may be obtained from the National Civic League, 1445 Market Street, Suite 300, Denver, Colorado 80202-1717.

LESSON THREE

MODEL REGIONAL GOVERNMENT CHARTER

Model Regional Government Charter

Metropolitan Service District

Filed by the Metro Charter Committee with the elections officer of the Portland area metropolitan service district, pursuant to ORS 268.730, and approved by district voters at the November 7, 1992 general election as amended by district voters at the November 7, 2000 general election.

PREAMBLE

We, the people of the Portland area metropolitan service district, in order to establish an elected, visible and accountable regional government that is responsive to the citizens of the region and works cooperatively with our local governments; that undertakes, as it most important service, planning and policy making to preserve and enhance the quality of life and the environment for ourselves and future generations; and that provides regional services needed and desired by the citizens in an efficient and effective manner, do ordain this charter for the Portland area metropolitan service district, to be known as Metro.

CHAPTER I – NAMES AND BOUNDARIES

Section 1. Title of Charter.
The title of this charter is the 1992 Metro Charter.

Section 2. Name of Regional Government.
The Portland area metropolitan service district, referred to in this charter as the "Metropolitan Service District," continues under this charter as a metropolitan service district with the name "Metro."

Section 3. Boundaries.
The Metro area of governance includes all territory within the boundaries of the Metropolitan Service District on the effective date of this charter and any territory later annexed or subjected to Metro governance under state law. This charter refers to that area as the "Metro area." Changes of Metro boundaries are not effective unless approved by ordinance. No change of Metro boundaries requires approval by a local government boundary commission or any other state agency unless required by law. The custodian of Metro records shall keep an accurate description of Metro boundaries and make it available for public inspection.

CHAPTER II – FUNCTIONS AND POWERS

Section 4. Jurisdiction of Metro.

Metro has jurisdiction over matters of the powers of metropolitan concern. Matters of metropolitan concern include the powers granted to and duties imposed on Metro by current and future state law and those matters the council by ordinance determines to be of metropolitan concern. The council shall specify by ordinance the extent to which Metro exercises jurisdiction over matters of metropolitan concern.

Section 5. Regional Planning Functions.

(1) Future Vision.

(a)   Adoption. The council shall adopt a Future Vision of the region between January 15, 1995 and July 1, 1995. The Future Vision is a conceptual statement that indicates population levels and settlement patterns that the region can accommodate within the carrying capacity of the land, water and air resources of the region, and its educational and economic resources, and that achieves a desired quality of life. The Future Vision is a long-term, visionary outlook for at least a 50-year period. As used in this section, "region" means the Metro area and adjacent area.

(b)   Matters addressed. The matters addressed by the Future Vision include but are not limited to: (a) use, restoration and preservation of regional land and natural resources for the benefit of present and future generations; (2) how and where to accommodate the population growth for the region while maintaining a desired quality of life for its residents; and (3) how to develop new communities and additions to the existing urban areas in well-planned ways.

(c)   Development. The council shall appoint a commission to develop and recommend a proposed Future Vision by a date the council sets. The commission shall be broadly representative of both public and private sectors, including the academic community, in the region. At least one member must reside outside the Metro area. The commission has authority to seek any necessary information and shall consider all relevant information and public comment in developing the proposed Future Vision. The commission serves without compensation.

(d)   Review and amendment. The Future Vision may be reviewed and amended as provided by ordinance. The Future Vision shall be completely reviewed and revised at least every fifteen years in the manner specified in subsection (1)(c) of this section.

(e)   Effect. The Future Vision is not a regulatory document. It is the intent of this charter that the Future Vision have no effect that would allow court or agency review it.

(2) Regional Framework Plan.

(a)   Adoption. The council shall adopt a regional framework plan by December 31, 1997 with the consultation and advice of the Metro Policy Advisory Committee (MPAC) created under section 27 of this charter. The council may adopt the regional framework plan in components.

(b) Matters addressed. The regional framework plan shall address: (1) regional transportation and mass transit systems; (2) management and amendment of the urban growth boundary; (3) protection of lands outside the urban growth boundary for natural resource, future urban or other uses; (4) housing densities; (5) urban design and settlement patterns; (6) parks, open spaces and recreational facilities; (7) water sources and storage; (8) coordination, to the extent feasible, of Metro growth management and land use planning policies with those of Clark County, Washington; and (9) planning responsibilities mandated by state law. The regional framework plan shall also address other growth management and land use planning matters which the council, with the consultation and advice of the MPAC, determines are of metropolitan concern and will benefit from regional planning. To encourage regional uniformity, the regional framework plan shall also contain model terminology, standards and procedures for local land use decision making that may be adopted by local governments. As used in this section, "local" refers only to the cities and counties within the jurisdiction of Metro.

(c) Effect. The regional framework plan shall: (1) describe its relationship to the Future Vision; (2) comply with applicable statewide planning goals; (3) be subject to compliance acknowledgment by the Land Conservation and Development Commission or its successor; and (4) be the basis for coordination of local comprehensive plans and implementing regulations.

(d) Amendment. The council may amend the regional framework plan after seeking the consultation and advice of the MPAC.

(e) Implementation. To the maximum extent allowed by law, the council shall adopt ordinances: (1) requiring local comprehensive plans and implementing regulations to comply with the regional framework plan within three years after adoption of the entire regional framework plan. If the regional framework plan is subject to compliance acknowledgment, local plans and implementing regulations shall be required to comply with the regional framework plan within two years of compliance acknowledgment; (2) requiring the council to adjudicate and determine the consistency of local comprehensive plans with the regional framework plan; (3) requiring each city and county within the jurisdiction of Metro to make local land use decisions consistent with the regional framework plan until its comprehensive plan has been determined to be consistent with the regional framework plan. The obligation to apply the regional framework plan to local land use decisions shall not begin until one year after adoption and compliance acknowledgment of the regional framework plan; and (4) allowing the council to require changes in local land use standards and procedures in the council determines changes are necessary to remedy a pattern or practice of decision making inconsistent with the regional framework plan.

(3) Priority and funding of regional planning activities. The regional planning functions under this section are the primary functions of Metro. The council shall appropriate funds sufficient to assure timely completion of those functions.

Section 6. Other Assigned Functions.

Other Assigned Functions. Metro is also authorized to exercise the following functions:

(1) Acquisition, development, maintenance and operation of: (a) a metropolitan zoo, (b) public cultural, trade, convention, exhibition, sports, entertainment, and spectator facilities, (c) facilities for the disposal of solid and liquid wastes, and (d) a system of parks, open spaces and recreational facilities of metropolitan concern; (2) disposal of solid and liquid wastes; (3) metropolitan aspects of natural disaster planning and response coordination; (4) development and marketing of data; and (5) any other function required by state law or assigned to the Metropolitan Service District or Metro by the voters.

Section 7. Assumption of Additional Functions.

(1) Assumption of ordinance. The council shall approve by ordinance the undertaking by Metro of any function not authorized by sections 5 and 6 of this charter. The ordinance shall contain a finding that the function is of metropolitan concern and the reasons it is appropriate for Metro to undertake it.

(2) Assumption of local government service function.

(a) An ordinance authorizing provision or regulation by Metro of a local government service Is not effective unless the ordinance is approved by the voters of Metro or a majority of the members of the MPAC. Voter approval may occur by approval of a referred measure (1) authorizing the function or (2) relating to finances and authorizing financing or identifying funds to be used for exercise of the function. As used in this section, "local government service" is a service provided to constituents by one or more cities, counties or special districts within the jurisdiction of Metro at the time a Metro ordinance on assumption of the service is first introduced.

(b) An ordinance submitted to the MPAC for approval is deemed approved unless disapproved within 60 days after submission.

(c) No approval under this subsection is required for the compensated provision of services by Metro to or on behalf of a local government under an agreement with that government.

(3) Assumption of other service functions. The council shall seek the advice of the MPAC before adopting an ordinance authorizing provision or regulation by Metro of a service, which is not a local government service.

(4) Assumption of functions and operation of mass transit district. Notwithstanding subsection (2) of this section, Metro may at any tine assume the duties, functions, powers and operations of a mass transit district by ordinance. Before adoption of this ordinance the council shall seek the

advice of the Joint Policy Advisory Committee on Transportation or its successor. After assuming the functions and operations of a mass transit district, the council shall establish a mass transit commission of not fewer than seven members and determine its duties in administering mass transit functions for Metro. The members of the governing body of the mass transit district at the time of its assumption by Metro are members of the initial Metro mass transit commission for the remainder of their respective terms of office.

(5) Boundary commission functions. The council shall undertake and complete a study of the Portland Metropolitan Area Local Government Boundary Commission, with advice of the MPAC, by September 1, 1995. The council shall implement the results of the study and shall seek any legislative action needed for implementation.

Section 8. Preservation of Authority to Contract.
All Metro officers shall preserve, to the greatest extent possible, the ability of Metro to contract for all services with persons or entities who are not Metro employees.

Section 9. General Grant of Powers to Carry Out Functions; Construction of Specified Powers.
When carrying out the functions authorized or assumed under this charter: (1) Metro has all powers that the laws of the United States and this state now or in the future could allow Metro just as if this charter specifically set out each of those powers; (2) the powers specified in this charter are not exclusive; (3) any specification of power in this charter is not intended to limit authority; and (4) the powers specified in this charter shall be construed liberally.

CHAPTER III – FINANCE

Section 10. General Authority.
Except as prohibited by law or restricted by this charter, Metro may impose, levy and collect taxes and may issue revenue bonds, general and special obligation bonds, certificates of participation and other obligations. The authority provided under this section supplements any authority otherwise granted by law.

Section 11. Voter Approval of Certain Taxes.
Any ordnance of the council imposing broadly based taxes of general applicability on the personal income, business income, payroll, property, or sales of goods or services of all, or a number of classes of, persons or entities in the region requires approval of the voters of Metro before taking effect. This approval is not required (1) to continue property taxes imposed by the Metropolitan Service District, (2) for the rate or amount of any payroll tax imposed by a mass transit district as of June 1, 1992, if the functions of that district are assumed by Metro, or (3) for additional payroll tax revenues for mass transit imposed to replace revenues lost by withdrawal of any locality from the service area of the mass transit district after June 1, 1992. For purposes of sections 11, 13, and

14 of this charter, "taxes" do not include any user charge, service fee, franchise fee, charge for the issuance of any franchise, license, permit or approval, or any benefit assessment against property.

Section 12. Voter Approval of General Obligation Bonds.

Issuance of general obligation bonds payable from ad valorem property taxes requires the approval of the voters of Metro.

Section 13. Prior Consultation for Tax Imposition.

Before imposing any new tax for which voter approval is not required, the council shall establish and seek the advice of a tax study committee that includes members appointed from the general population, and from among businesses and governments of cities, counties, special districts, and school districts, of the Metro area.

Section 14. Limitations of Expenditures of Certain Tax Revenues.

(1) Generally. Except as provided in this section, for the first fiscal year after this charter takes effect Metro may make no more that $12,500,000 in expenditures on a cash basis from taxes imposed and received by Metro and interest and other earnings on those taxes. This expenditure limitation increases in each subsequent fiscal year by a percentage equal to (a) the rate of increase in the Consumer Price Index, All Items, for Portland-Vancouver (All Urban Consumers) as determined by the appropriate federal agency or (b) the most nearly equivalent index as determined by the council if the index in (a) is discontinued.

(2) Exclusions from limitation. This section does not apply to (a) taxes approved by the voters of Metro or any Metropolitan Service District and interest and other earnings on those taxes, (b) payroll taxes specified in Section 11 of this charter, and (c) tax increment financing charges on property.

Section 15. Limitations on Amount of User Charges.

Except to the extent receipts in excess of costs from food and beverage sales, parking and other concessions are dedicated to reducing charges for the provision of goods or services to which the concession directly relates, charges for the provision of goods or services by Metro may not exceed the costs of providing the goods or services. These costs include, but are not limited to, costs of personal service, materials, capital outlay, debt service, operating expenses, overhead expenses, and capital and operational reserves attributable to the goods or services.

CHAPTER IV – FORM OF GOVERNMENT

Section 16. Metro Council.

(1) Creation and Powers. The Metro council is created as the governing body of Metro. Except as this charter provides otherwise, and except for initiative and referendum powers reserved to the voters of Metro, all Metro powers are vested in the council.

(2) Composition. Beginning January 6, 2003, the council consists of seven (7) councilors, one of whom shall be elected at large and designate President of the council and six (6) each nominated and elected from a single district within the Metro area. Until that date the council consists of the seven (7) members of the Metro Council whose terms begin or continue in January 2001 and whose districts continue until replaced.

(3) Initial terms of office. The terms of office of the four councilors receiving the highest number of votes among the seven councilors elected in 1994 end January 4, 1999. The terms of office of the other three councilors end January 6, 1997. Thereafter the term of office of councilor is four years.

(4) Presiding Officer, Council President.

(a)   Presiding Officer. At its first meeting each year before 2003, the council shall elect a presiding officer from its councilors.

(b)   Council President. The Council President presides over the Council. The Council President sets the council agenda subject to general rules established by a council adopted ordinance. Except as provided otherwise by the Metro Charter, the Council President appoints all members of the committees, commissions and boards created by the rules of the council and ordinances of Metro.

(5) Annual Organizing Resolution. At the first Council meeting each January the Council shall adopt an annual organizing resolution naming a deputy and establish such committees as the Council deems necessary for the orderly conduct of council business.

(6) Council meetings. The council shall meet regularly in the Metro area at times and places it designates. The council shall prescribe by ordinance the rules to govern conduct of its meetings. Except as this charter provides otherwise, the agreement of a majority of councilors present and constituting a quorum is necessary to decide affirmatively a question before the council.

(7) Quorum. A majority of councilors in office is a quorum for council business, but fewer councilors may compel absent councilors to attend.

(8) Record of proceedings. The council shall keep and authenticate a record of council proceedings.

Section 17. Metro Executive Officer.

(1) Creation. The office of Metro executive officer is created. The executive officer is elected from the Metro area at large for a term of four years. The executive officer serves full time and may not be employed by any other person or entity while serving as executive officer.

(2) Duties. The primary duty of the executive officer is to enforce Metro ordinances and otherwise to execute the policies of the council. The executive officer shall also: (a) administer Metro except for the council and the auditor; (b) make appointments to Metro offices boards, commissions

and committees when required to do so by this charter of by ordinance; (c) propose for council adoption measures deemed necessary to enforce of carry out powers and duties of Metro; (d) prepare and submit a recommended annual Metro budget to the council for approval; and (e) keep the council fully advised about Metro operations.

(3) Transition from Metropolitan Service District. The Metropolitan Service District executive officer in office when this charter takes effect is the Metro executive officer until January 2, 1995 when his or her term expires. The Metro executive officer is elected in the first statewide primary or general election after adoption of this charter for a term beginning January 2, 1995.

(4) Veto.

(a) Except a provided in this subsection, the executive officer may veto the following legislative acts of the council within five business days after enactment: (1) any annual or supplemental Metro budget, (2) any ordinance imposing, or providing a exception from, a tax, and (3) any ordinance imposing a charge for provision of goods, services or property by Metro, franchise fees or any assessment.

(b) The council, not later than 30 days after a veto, may override a veto by the affirmative vote of (1) nine councilors while the council consists of 13 positions and (2) five councilors after the council consists of seven positions as provided by section 16(2) of this charter.

(c) A legislative act referred to the voters of Metro by the council is not subject to veto.

(5) Office Abolished. Effective January 6, 2003, the office of the Executive Officer is abolished.

(6) Section 17 Repealed. Section 17 of the Metro Charter is repealed January 6, 2003. Upon repeal, its provisions shall be stricken from the Metro Charter.

Section 18. Metro Auditor.
(1) Creation. The office of Metro auditor is created. The auditor is elected from the Metro area at large for a term of four years. The auditor serves full time and may not be employed by any-other person or entity while serving as auditor.

(2) First election; disqualification for other Metro elected offices. The auditor is first elected in the first statewide primary or general election after adoption of this charter for a term beginning January 2, 1995. During the term for which elected, and for four years thereafter, the auditor is ineligible to hold the office of Metro councilor.

(3) Duties. The auditor shall: (a) make continuous investigations of the operations of Metro including financial and performance auditing and review of financial transactions, personnel, equipment, facilities, and all other aspects of those operations, and (b) make reports to the Metro council of the results of any investigation with any recommendation for remedial action. Except as provided in this section, the auditor may not be given responsibility to perform any executive function.

Section 19. Term of Office.

The term of office of an officer elected at a primary or general election begins the first Monday of the year following election and continues until a successor assumes the office.

CHAPTER V – OFFICERS, COMMISSIONS, AND EMPLOYEES

Section 20. Qualifications of Elected Officers.

(1) Councilor. A councilor shall be a qualified elector under the constitution of this state when his or her term of office begins and shall have resided during the preceding 12 months in the district from which elected or appointed. When the boundaries of that district have been apportioned or reapportioned during that period, residency in that district for purposes of this subsection includes residency in any former district with area in the district from which the councilor is elected or appointed if residence is established in the apportioned or reapportioned district within 60 days after the apportionment or reapportionment is effective.

(2) Council President and auditor. The Council President and auditor shall each be a qualified elector under the constitution of this state when his or her term of office begins and shall have resided during the preceding 12 months within the boundaries of Metro as they exist when the term of office begins. At the time of election or appointment, the auditor shall also hold the designation of certified public accountant or certified internal auditor.

(3) Multiple elected offices. A Metro elected officer may not be an elected officer of the state, or a city, county or special district during his or her term of office. As used in this charter, special district does not include school districts.

(4) Judging elections and qualifications. The council is the judge of the election and qualification of its members.

Section 21. Compensation of Elected Officers.

(1) Council. Prior to 2003, the salary of the presiding officer is two-thirds the salary of a circuit court judge of this state and salary of every other councilor is one-third the salary of circuit court judge of this state. Beginning January 6, 2003, the salary of the Council President shall be that of a circuit court judge of this state and the salary of every other councilor is one-third the salary of a circuit court judge. A councilor may waive a salary.

(2) Executive officer. Until the office is abolished, the salary of the executive officer is the salary of a circuit court judge of this state.

(3) Auditor. The salary of the auditor is eighty percent the salary of a circuit court judge of this state.

(4) Full Compensation. Elected officers compensation, as established by this charter, shall be the elected officers full and exclusive compensation for their duties as Metro officers or for any

duties or responsibilities resulting from their position. This Section does not preclude elected officers from receiving ordinary employee fringe benefits or being reimbursed for any actual and reasonable expenses recurred by an elected officer in the course of performing official duties.

Section 22. Oath.

Before assuming office a Metro elected officer shall take an oath or affirm that he or she will faithfully perform the duties of the office and support the constitutions and laws of the United States and this state and the charter and laws of Metro.

Section 23. Vacancies in Office.

(1) Councilor. The office of councilor becomes vacant upon the incumbent's: (a) death, (b) adjudicated incompetency, (c) recall from office, (d) failure following election or appointment to qualify for the office within 10 days after the time for his or her term of office to begin, (e) absence from all meetings of the council within a 60 day period without the council's consent,

(f) ceasing to reside in the district from which elected or appointed, except when district boundaries are reapportioned and a councilor is assigned to a district where the councilor does not reside and the councilor becomes a resident of the reapportioned district within 60 days after the reapportionment is effective, (g) ceasing to be a qualified elector under state law, (h) conviction of a felony or conviction of a federal or state offense punishable by loss of liberty and pertaining to his or her office, (i) resignation from office, or (j) becoming an elected officer of the state or a city, county or special district.

(2) Council President and auditor. The offices of Council President or auditor become vacant in the circumstances described in subsection (a)-(d) and (g)-(j) of this section, or if the Council President or auditor ceases to reside in the Metro area. The office of auditor also becomes vacant if the incumbent ceases to hold the designation of certified public accountant or certified internal auditor.

(3) Vacancy after reapportionment. If a councilor vacancy occurs after the councilor has been assigned to a reapportioned district under section 32 of this charter, the vacancy is in the district to which that councilor was assigned.

(4) Determination of vacancy. The council is the final judge of the existence of a vacancy.

Section 24. Filling Vacancies.

A majority of councilors holding office shall fill a vacancy by appointment within 90 days after it occurs. The term of office of the appointee runs from the time he or she qualifies for the office after appointment until a successor is duly elected and qualifies for the office. If the vacancy occurs more than 20 days before the first general election after the beginning of the term that office, the term of office of the appointee runs only until the first council meeting in the year immediately after that election. A person shall be elected for the remainder of the term at the first primary or general election after the beginning of the term.

Section 25. Limitations of Terms of Office.

No person may be elected councilor for more than three consecutive full terms, not including any term or terms as Council President. No person may be elected Council President for more than two consecutive full terms. Any term served as Executive Officer shall be considered as a term served as Council President. The limitations of this section apply only to terms of office beginning on or after January 2, 1995.

Section 26. Appointive Offices and Commissions.

(1) Chief Operating Officer. The Council shall provide by ordinance for the creation of the office of the Chief Operating Officer. The Chief Operating Officer's duties and responsibilities will be more specifically established by ordinance. The Council President appoints the Chief Operating Officer subject to confirmation by the Council. The Chief Operating Officer serves at the pleasure of the Council and is subject to removal by the Council President with the concurrence of the Council.

(2) Metro Attorney. The Council shall provide by ordinance for the creation of the office of Metro Attorney. The Council President appoints the Metro Attorney subject to the confirmation of the Council. The metro Attorney serves at the pleasure of the Council and is subject to removal by the Council President with the concurrence of the Council.

(3) Other Offices. The Council may provide by ordinance for the creation of other offices not subordinate to the Chief Operating Officer. The duties and responsibilities of these offices will be more specifically established by ordinance. The Council President appoints all other officers subject confirmation by the Council. All other officers serve at the pleasure of the Council and are subject to removal by the Council President with the concurrence of the Council.

(4) Commissions. The Council may by ordinance create Commissions with duties and responsibilities as specified by the Council. The Council President appoints all Commissioners subject to confirmation by the Council. Commissioners serve at the pleasure of the Council and are subject to removal by the Council President with the concurrence of the Council.

Section 27. Metro Policy Advisory Committee.

(1) Creation and composition. The Metro Policy Advisory Committee (MPAC) is created. The initial members of the MPAC are:

   (a)   One member of each of the governing bodies of Washington, Clackamas and Multnomah Counties appointed by the body from which the member is chosen;
   (b)   Two members of the governing body of the City of Portland appointed by that governing body;

(c)   One member of the governing body of the second largest city in population in Multnomah County appointed by that governing body;

(d)   One member of the governing body of the largest city in population in Washington County appointed by that governing body

(e)   One member of the governing body of the largest city in population in Clackamas County appointed by that governing body;

(f)   One member of a governing body of a city with territory in the Metro area of Multnomah County other than either the City of Portland or the second largest city in population in Multnomah County, appointed jointly by the governing bodies of cities with territory in the Metro area of Multnomah County other than the City of Portland or the second largest city in population in Multnomah County;

(g)   One member of a governing body of a city with territory in the Metro area of Washington County other than the city in Washington County with the largest population, appointed jointly by the governing bodies of cities with territory in the Metro area in Washington County other than the city in Washington County with the largest population;

(h)   One member of a governing body of a city with territory in the Metro area in Clackamas County other than the city in Clackamas County with the largest population, appointed jointly by the governing bodies of cities with territory in the Metro area in Clackamas County other than the city in Clackamas County with the largest population;

(i)   One member from the governing body of a special district with territory in the Metro area in Multnomah County appointed jointly by the governing bodies of special districts with territory in the Metro area in Multnomah County;

(j)   One member from the governing body of a special district with territory in the Metro area in Washington County appointed jointly by the governing bodies of special districts with territory in the Metro area in Washington County;

(k)   One member from the governing body of a special district with territory in the Metro area of Clackamas County appointed jointly by the governing bodies of special districts with territory in the Metro area in Clackamas County;

(l)   One member of the governing body of Tri-County Metropolitan Transportation District of Oregon appointed by the governing body of that district; and

(m)   Three persons appointed by the Council President and confirmed by the council. No person appointed under this part of subsection (1) may be an elected officer of or employed by Metro, the state or a city, county or special district. Each person appointed under this part of subsection (1) shall reside in the Metro area during the person's tenure on the MPAC.

(2) Change of composition. A vote of both a majority of the MPAC members and a majority of all councilors may change the composition of the MPAC at any time.

(3) Duties. The MPAC shall perform the duties assigned to it by this charter and any other duties the council prescribes.

(4) Bylaws. The MPAC shall adopt bylaws governing the conduct and record of its meetings and the terms of its members.

Section 28. Metro Office of Citizen Involvement.

(1) Creation and purpose. The Metro office of citizen involvement is created to develop and maintain programs and procedures to aid communication between citizens and the council.

(2) Citizens' committee in office of citizen involvement. The council shall establish by ordinance (a) a citizens' committee in the office of citizen involvement and (b) a citizen involvement process. The council shall appropriate sufficient funds to operate the office and committee.

CHAPTER VI – ELECTIONS AND REAPPORTIONMENT

Section 29. State Law.

Except as this charter or a Metro ordinance provides otherwise, a Metro election shall conform to state law applicable to the election.

Section 30. Elections of Metro Officers.

(1) Generally. Except for certain elections to fill a vacancy in office, the first vote for councilor, council president or auditor occurs at an election held at the same time and places in the Metro area as the statewide primary election that year. If one candidate for a Metro office receives a majority of the votes cast at the primary elections for all candidates for that office, the candidate is elected. If no candidate receives a majority of the votes cast at the primary election, the candidates receiving the two largest number of votes cast for the office are the only names to appear on the general election ballot that year as candidates for that office.

(2) Nonpartisan offices. All elections for Metro officers are nonpartisan. Election ballots shall list the names of candidates for Metro offices without political party designations.

Section 31. Multiple Candidacies.

No person may be a candidate at a single election for more than one Metro elected office.

Section 32. Reapportionment of Council Districts After Census.

(1) General requirements. Within three months after an official census indicates that the boundaries of council districts deny equal protection of the law, the council shall change the boundaries to accord equal protection of the law and shall assign councilors to the reapportioned districts. As nearly as practicable, all council districts shall be of equal population and each shall be contiguous and geographically compact. The council may by ordinance specify additional criteria for districts that are consistent with the section.

(2) Failure to reapportion. If the council fails to establish council district boundaries as provided by this section, the council president shall establish the boundaries within 60 days.

(3) Redistricting After Year 2000 Census. Within three (3) months after completion of the year 2000 Census, the Council shall establish six (6) council districts in a manner that accords equal protection of the law. The three (3) councilors serving terms that expire in January 2005 shall each be assigned to one of the six (6) districts and their terms shall continue. Council members will be elected to serve four (4) year terms for the other three (3) districts in the regularly scheduled elections to be held in 2002. For the purpose of Section 33 of this charter, the seven (7) councilors in office in January 2001 shall be deemed to be serving in the districts from which they were elected until January 2003.

Section 33. Recall.

(1) Generally. An elected officer of Metro may be recalled in the manner and with the effect described by the constitution and laws of this state.

(2) Effect of reapportionment. Upon the effective date of a council reapportionment under Section 32 of this charter, a councilor is subject to recall by the voters of the district to which the councilor is assigned and not by the voters of the district of that councilor existing before the reapportionment.

Section 34. Initiative and Referendum.

The voters of Metro reserve to themselves the powers of initiative and referendum. The council may provide for the exercise of those powers in a manner consistent with law.

Section 35. Amendment and Revision of Charter.

The council may refer, and voters of Metro may initiate, amendments to this charter. A proposed charter amendment may embrace on one subject and matters properly connected with it. The council shall provide by ordinance for a procedure to revise this charter.

CHAPTER VII – ORDINANCES

Section 36. Ordaining Clause.

The ordaining clause of an ordinance adopted by the council is: "The Metro Council ordains as follows:." The ordaining clause of an initiated or referred ordinance is: "The People of Metro ordain as follows:."

Section 37. Adoption by Council.

(1) General Requirements. The council shall adopt all legislation of Metro by ordinance. Except as this charter otherwise provides, the council may not adopt any ordinance at a meeting unless: (a) the ordinance is introduced at a previous meeting of the council, (b) the title of the ordinance is included in a written agenda of the meeting at which the ordinance is adopted, (c) the agenda of that meeting is publicized not less than three business days nor more than ten days before the meeting, and (d) copies of the ordinance are available for public inspection at least three business

days before that meeting. The text of an ordinance may be amended, but not substantially revised, at the meeting at which it is adopted.

(2) Immediate adoption. The provisions of this section do not apply to an ordinance adopted by unanimous consent of the council and containing findings on the need for immediate adoption.

(3) Vote required. Adoption of an ordinance requires the affirmative votes of (a) seven councilors while the council consists of 13 positions, (b) four councilors after the council consists of seven positions as provided by Section 16(2) of this charter.

Section 38. Endorsement.

The person presiding over the council when an ordinance is adopted shall endorse the ordinance unless the council prescribes a different procedure by general ordinance.

Section 39. Effective Date of Ordinances.

(1) Generally. An ordinance takes effect 90 days after its adoption unless the ordinance states a different effective date. An ordinance may state an earlier effective date if (a) an earlier date is necessary for the health, safety or welfare of the Metro area; (b) the reasons why this is so are stated in an emergency clause of the ordinance; and (c) the ordinance is approved by the affirmative vote of two-thirds of all councilors. An ordinance imposing or changing a tax or charge, changing the boundaries of Metro, or assuming a function may not contain an emergency clause.

(2) Referred ordinances. If the council refers an ordinance to the voters of Metro, the ordinance effective date is the 30th day after its approval by a majority of the voters voting on the measure unless the ordinance specifies a later date. If a referendum petition is filed with the filing officer not later than the 90th day after adoption of an ordinance, the ordinance effective date is suspended. An ordinance is not subject to the referendum after it is effective. An ordinance referred by a referendum petition (a) does not take effect if a majority of the voters voting on the measure reject it and (b) takes effect, unless the ordinance specifies a later date, on the date the results of the election are certified if a majority of the voters voting on the measure approve it.

Section 40. Content of Ordinances.

Each ordinance may embrace only one subject and all matters properly connected with it. The council shall plainly word each ordinance and avoid technical terms as far as practicable.

Section 41. Public Improvements and Special Assessments.

General ordinances govern the procedures for making, altering, vacating or abandoning a public improvement and for fixing, levying and collecting special assessments against real property for public improvements or services. State law governs these procedures to the extent not governed by general ordinances.

CHAPTER VIII – MISCELLANEOUS PROVISIONS

Section 42. Transition Provisions.

All legislation, orders, rules and regulations of the Metropolitan Service District in force when this charter takes effect remain in force after that time to the extent consistent with is charter and until amended or repealed by the council. All rights, claims, causes of action, duties, contracts, and legal and administrative proceedings of the Metropolitan Service District that exist when this charter takes effect continue and are unimpaired by the charter. Each is in the charge of the officer or agency designated by this charter or by its authority to have charge of it. The unexpired terms of elected officers of the Metropolitan Service District continue as provided by this charter. Upon the effective date of this charter, the assets and liabilities of the Metropolitan Service District are the assets and liabilities of Metro.

Section 43. Effective Date.

This charter takes effect January 1, 1993.

Section 44. Severability.

The terms of this charter are severable. If a part of this charter is held invalid, that invalidity does not affect any other part of this charter unless required by the logical relation between the parts.

Section 45. State Legislation.

By adopting this charter the voters of Metro direct the council to seek, and request the Legislative Assembly of this state to enact, any legislation needed to make all parts of this charter operative.

Section 46. Further Transition Provisions.

The amendment to Sections 16(4)(b), 16(5), 18, 20, 23, 26, 27, 28, 32(2) and 39 adopted by the electors of Metro at the November 2000 election take effect of January 6, 2003.[1]

– – – –

Editor's Note: Additional information may be obtained from the Metropolitan Service District, 600 NE Grand Avenue, Portland, Oregon 97232-2736.

– – – –

Notes

1   Voters approved the Metropolitan Service District's ("Metro's") original home-rule charter in 1992, and amendments to this charter in the November 2000 election. Prior to 1992, Metro's structure and responsibilities were laid out by the Oregon Legislature.

LESSON FOUR

MODEL STATE GOVERNMENT CHARTER

Model State Government Charter

Council of State Governments

PREAMBLE

We, the people of the state of _____, recognizing the rights and duties of this state as a part of the federal system of government, reaffirm our adherence to the Constitution of the United States of America; and in order to assure the state government power to act for the good order of the state and the liberty, health, safety and welfare of the people, we do ordain and establish this constitution.

ARTICLE I
Bill of Rights

Section 1.01. *Freedom of Religion, Speech, Press, Assembly and Petition.* No law shall be enacted respecting an establishment of religion, or prohibiting the free exercise thereof, or abridging the freedom of speech or of the press, or the right of the people peaceably to assemble and to petition the government for a redress of grievances.

Section 1.02. *Due Process and Equal Protection.* No person shall be deprived of life, liberty or property without due process of law, nor be denied the equal protection of the laws, nor be denied the enjoyment of his civil rights or be discriminated against in the exercise thereof because of race, national origin, religion or ancestry.

Section 1.03. *Searches and Seizures and Interceptions.*

(a) The right of the people to be secure in their persons, houses, papers and effects against unreasonable searches and seizures shall not be violated, and no warrants shall issue, but upon probable cause, supported by oath or affirmation, and particularly describing the place to be searched and the persons or things to be seized.

(b) The right of the people to be secure against unreasonable interception of telephone, telegraph and other electronic means of communication, and against unreasonable interception of oral and other communications by electric or electronic methods, shall not be violated, and no orders and warrants for such interceptions shall issue but upon probable cause supported by oath or affirmation that evidence of crime may be thus obtained, and particularly identifying the means of communication and the person or persons whose communications are to be intercepted.

(c) Evidence obtained in violation of this section shall not be admissible in any court against any person.

Section 1.04. *Self-Incrimination.* No person shall be compelled to give testimony which might tend to incriminate him.

Section 1.05. *Writ of Habeas Corpus.* The privilege of the writ of habeas corpus shall not be suspended unless when in cases of rebellion or invasion the public safety may require it.

Section 1.06. *Rights of Accused Persons.*

(a) In all criminal prosecutions the accused shall enjoy the right to a speedy and public trial, to be informed of the nature and cause of the accusation, to be confronted with the witnesses against him, to have compulsory process for obtaining witnesses in his favor, to have the assistance of counsel for his defense, and to the assignment of counsel to represent him at every stage of the proceedings unless he elects to proceed without counsel or is able to obtain counsel. In prosecutions for felony, the accused shall also enjoy the right of trial by an impartial jury of the county [or other appropriate political subdivision of the state] wherein the crime shall have been committed, or of another county, if a change of venue has been granted.

(b) All persons shall, before conviction, be bailable by sufficient sureties, but bail may be denied to persons charged with capital offenses or offenses punishable by life imprisonment, giving due weight to the evidence and to the nature and circumstances of the event. Excessive bail shall not be required, nor excessive fines imposed, nor cruel or unusual punishment inflicted.

(c) No person shall be twice put in jeopardy for the same offense.

Section 1.07. *Political Tests for Public Office.* No oath, declaration or political test shall be required for any public office or employment other than the following oath or affirmation: "I do solemnly swear [or affirm] that I will support and defend the Constitution of the United States and the constitution of the state of _____ and that I will faithfully discharge the duties of the office of _____ to the best of my ability."

ARTICLE II
Powers of the State

Section 2.01. *Powers of Government.* The enumeration in this constitution of specified powers and functions shall be construed neither as a grant nor as a limitation of the powers of state government but the state government shall have all of the powers not denied by this constitution or by or under the Constitution of the United States.

ARTICLE III
Suffrage and Elections

Section 3.01. *Qualifications for Voting.* Every citizen of the age of _____ years and a resident of the state for three months shall have the right to vote in the election of all officers that may be elected by the people and upon all questions that may be submitted to the voters; but the legislature may by law establish: (1) Minimum periods of local residence not exceeding three months, (2) reasonable requirements to determine literacy in English or in another language predominantly used in the classrooms of any public or private school accredited by any state or territory of the United States, the District of Columbia, or the Commonwealth of Puerto Rico, and (3) disqualifications for voting for mental incompetency or conviction of felony.

Section 3.02. *Legislature to Prescribe for Exercise of Suffrage.* The legislature shall by law define residence for voting purposes, insure secrecy in voting and provide for the registration of voters, absentee voting, the administration of elections and the nomination of candidates.

ARTICLE IV
The Legislature

Section 4.01. *Legislative Power.* The legislative power of the state shall be vested in the legislature.

Section 4.02. *Composition of the Legislature.* The legislature shall be composed of a single chamber consisting of one member to represent each legislative district. The number of members shall be prescribed by law but shall not be less than _____ nor exceed _____. Each member of the legislature shall be a qualified voter of the state and shall be at least _____ years of age.

> BICAMERAL ALTERNATIVE: Section 4.02. *Composition of the Legislature.* The legislature shall be composed of a senate and an assembly. The number of members of each house of the legislature shall be prescribed by law but the number of assemblymen shall not be less than _____ nor exceed _____, and the number of senators shall not exceed one-third, as near as may be, the number of assemblymen. Each assemblyman shall represent one assembly district and each senator shall represent one senate district. Each member of the legislature shall be a qualified voter of the state and shall be at least _____ years of age.

Section 4.03. *Election and Term of Members.* The members of the legislature shall be elected by the qualified voters of the state for a term of two years.

> BICAMERAL ALTERNATIVE: Section 4.03. *Election and Terms of Members.* Assemblymen shall be elected by the qualified voters of the state for a term of two years and senators for a term of six years. One-third of the senators shall be elected every two years.

Section 4.04. *Legislative Districts.*

(a) For the purpose of electing members of the legislature, the state shall be divided into as many districts as there shall be members of the legislature. Each district shall consist of compact and contiguous territory. All districts shall be so nearly equal in population that the population of the largest district shall not exceed that of the smallest district by more than _____ per cent.

In determining the population of each district, inmates of such public or private institutions as prisons or other places of correction, hospitals for the insane or other institutions housing persons who are disqualified from voting by law shall not be counted.

(b) Immediately following each decennial census, the governor shall appoint a board of _____ qualified voters to make recommendations within ninety days of their appointment concerning the redistricting of the state. The governor shall publish the recommendations of the board when received. The governor shall promulgate a redistricting plan within ninety to one hundred and twenty days after appointment of the board, whether or not it has made its recommendations. The governor shall accompany his plan with a message explaining his reasons for any changes from the recommendations of the board. The governor's redistricting plan shall be published in the manner provided for acts of the legislature and shall have the force of law upon such publication. Upon the application of any qualified voter, the supreme court, in the exercise of original, exclusive and final jurisdiction, shall review the governor's redistricting plan and shall have jurisdiction to make orders to amend the plan to comply with the requirements of this constitution or, if the governor has failed to promulgate a redistricting plan within the time provided, to make one or more orders establishing such a plan.

BICAMERAL ALTERNATIVE: Section 4.04. *Legislative Districts.*

(a) For the purpose of electing members of the assembly, the state shall be divided into as many districts as there shall be members of the assembly. Each district shall consist of compact and contiguous territory. All districts shall be so nearly equal in population that the district with the greatest population shall not exceed the district with the least population by more than _____ per cent. In determining the population of each district, inmates of such public or private institutions as prisons or other places of correction, hospitals for the insane or other institutions housing persons who are disqualified from voting by law shall not be counted.

(b) For the purpose of electing members of the senate, the state shall be divided into as many districts as there shall be members of the senate. Each senate district shall consist of a compact and contiguous territory. All districts shall be so nearly equal in population that the district with the greatest population shall not exceed the district with the least population by more than _____ per cent. In determining the population of each district, inmates of such public or private institutions as prisons or other places of correction, hospitals for the insane or other institutions housing persons who are disqualified from voting by law shall not be counted.

(c) Immediately following each decennial census, the governor shall appoint a board of _____ qualified voters to make recommendations within ninety days of their appointment concerning the redistricting of the state. The governor shall publish the recommendations of the board when received. The governor shall promulgate a redistricting plan within ninety to one hundred and twenty days after appointment of the board, whether or not it has made its recommendations. The governor shall accompany his plan with a message explaining his reasons for any changes from the recommendations of the board. The governor's redistricting plan shall be published in the manner provided for acts of the legislature and shall have the force of law upon such publication. Upon the application of any qualified voter, the supreme court, in the exercise of original, exclusive and final jurisdiction, shall review the governor's redistricting plan and shall have jurisdiction to make orders to amend the plan to comply with the requirements of this constitution or, if the governor has failed to promulgate a redistricting plan within the time provided, to make one or more orders establishing such a plan.

Section 4.05. *Time of Election.* Members of the legislature shall be elected at the regular election in each odd-numbered year.

Section 4.06. *Vacancies.* When a vacancy occurs in the legislature it shall be filled as provided by law.

Section 4.07. *Compensation of Members.* The members of the legislature shall receive an annual salary and such allowances as may be prescribed by law but any increase or decrease in the amount thereof shall not apply to the legislature which enacted the same.

Section 4.08. *Sessions.* The legislature shall be a continuous body during the term for which its members are elected. It shall meet in regular sessions annually as provided by law. It may be convened at other times by the governor or, at the written request of a majority of the members, by the presiding officer of the legislature.

> BICAMERAL ALTERNATIVE: Section 4.08. *Sessions.* The legislature shall be a continuous body during the term for which members of the assembly are elected. The legislature shall meet in regular sessions annually as provided by law. It may be convened at other times by the governor or, at the written request of a majority of the members of each house, by the presiding officers of both houses.

Section 4.09. *Organization and Procedure.* The legislature shall be the final judge of the election and qualifications of its members and may by law vest in the courts the trial and determination of contested elections of members. It shall choose its presiding officer from among its members and it shall employ a secretary to serve for an indefinite term. It shall determine its rules of procedure; it may compel the attendance of absent members, discipline its members and, with the concurrence of two-thirds of all the members, expel a member, and it shall have power to compel the attendance and testimony of witnesses and the production of books and papers either before the legislature as a whole or before any committee thereof. The secretary of the legislature shall be its chief fiscal, administrative and personnel officer and shall perform such duties as the legislature may prescribe.

> BICAMERAL ALTERNATIVE: Section 4.09. *Organization and Procedure.* Each house of the legislature shall be the final judge of the election and qualifications of its members and the

legislature may by law vest in the courts the trial and determination of contested elections of members. Each house of the legislature shall choose its presiding officer from among its members and it shall employ a secretary to serve for an indefinite term, and each house shall determine its rules of procedure; it may compel the attendance of absent members, discipline its members and, with the concurrence of two-thirds of all the members, expel a member, and it shall have power to compel the attendance and testimony of witnesses and the production of books and papers either before such house of the legislature as a whole or before any committee thereof. The secretary of each house of the legislature shall be its chief fiscal, administrative and personnel officer and shall perform such duties as each such house of the legislature may prescribe.

Section 4.10. *Legislative Immunity.* For any speech or debate in the legislature, the members shall not be questioned in any other place.

Section 4.11. *Special Legislation.* The legislature shall pass no special or local act when a general act is or can be made applicable, and whether a general act is or can be made applicable shall be a matter for judicial determination.

Section 4.12. *Transaction of Business.* A majority of all the members of the legislature shall constitute a quorum to do business but a smaller number may adjourn from day to day and compel the attendance of absent members. The legislature shall keep a journal of its proceedings which shall be published from day to day. The legislature shall prescribe the methods of voting on legislative matters but a record vote, with the yeas and nays entered in the journal, shall be taken on any question on the demand of one-fifth of the members present.

> BICAMERAL ALTERNATIVE: Section 4.12. *Transaction of Business.* Refer to "each house of the legislature" instead of "the legislature" wherever appropriate.

Section 4.13. *Committees.* The legislature may establish such committees as it may deem necessary for the conduct of its business. When a committee to which a bill has been assigned has not reported on it, one-third of all the members of the legislature shall have power to relieve it of further consideration. Adequate public notice of all committee hearings, with a clear statement of all subjects to be considered at each hearing, shall be published in advance.

> BICAMERAL ALTERNATIVE: Section 4.13. *Committees.* Refer to "each house of the legislature" instead of "the legislature" wherever appropriate.

Section 4.14. *Bills; Single Subject.* The legislature shall enact no law except by bill and every bill except bills for appropriations and bills for the codification, revision or rearrangement of existing laws shall be confined to one subject. All appropriation bills shall be limited to the subject of appropriations. Legislature compliance with the requirements of this section is a constitutional responsibility not subject to judicial review.

Section 4.15. *Passage of Bills.* No bill shall become a law unless it has been printed and upon the desks of the members in final form at least three days prior to final passage and the majority of all the members has assented to it. The yeas and nays on final passage shall be entered in the journal. The legislature shall provide for the publication of all acts and no act shall become effective until published as provided by law.

> BICAMERAL ALTERNATIVE: Section 4.15. *Passage of Bills.* Refer to "each house of the legislature" instead of "the legislature" wherever appropriate.

Section 4.16. *Action by the Governor.*

(a) When a bill has passed the legislature, it shall be presented to the governor and, if the legislature is in session, it shall become law if the governor either signs or fails to veto it within fifteen days of presentation. If the legislature is in recess or, if the session of the legislature has expired during such fifteen-day period, it shall become law if he signs it within thirty days after such adjournment or expiration. If the governor does not approve a bill, he shall veto it and return it to the legislature either within fifteen days of presentation if the legislature is in session or upon the reconvening of the legislature from its recess. Any bill so returned by the governor shall be reconsidered by the legislature, and, if upon reconsideration two-thirds of all the members shall agree to pass the bill, it shall become law.

(b) The governor may strike out or reduce items in appropriation bills passed by the legislature and the procedure in such cases shall be the same as in case of the disapproval of an entire bill by the governor.

> BICAMERAL ALTERNATIVE: Section 4.16. *Action by the Governor.* Refer to "each house of the legislature" instead of "the legislature" wherever appropriate.

Section 4.17. *Post-Audit.* The legislature shall appoint an auditor to serve at its pleasure. The auditor shall conduct post-audits as prescribed by law and shall report to the legislature and to the governor.

> BICAMERAL ALTERNATIVE: Section 4.17. *Post-Audit.* The legislature shall, by joint resolution, appoint … .

Section 4.18. *Impeachment.* The legislature may impeach the governor, the heads of principal departments, judicial officers and such other officers of the state as may be made subject to impeachment by law, by a two-thirds vote of all the members, and shall provide by law procedures for the trial and removal from office, after conviction, of officers so impeached. No officer shall be convicted on impeachment by a vote of less than two-thirds of the members of the tribunal hearing the charges.

> BICAMERAL ALTERNATIVE: Section 4.18. *Impeachment.* Refer to "by a two-thirds vote of all the members of each house."

ARTICLE V
The Executive

Section 5.01. *Executive Power.* The executive power of the state shall be vested in a governor.

Section 5.02. *Election and Qualifications of Governor.* The governor shall be elected, at the regular election every other odd-numbered year, by the direct vote of the people, for a term of four years beginning on the first day of [December] [January] next following his election. Any qualified voter of the state who is at least _____ years of age shall be eligible to the office of governor.

Section 5.03. *Governor's Messages to the Legislature.* The governor shall, at the beginning of each session, and may, at other times, give to the legislature information as to the affairs of the state and recommend measures he considers necessary or desirable.

Section 5.04. *Executive and Administrative Powers.*

(a) The governor shall be responsible for the faithful execution of the laws. He may, by appropriate action or proceeding brought in the name of the state, enforce compliance with any constitutional or legislative mandate, or restrain violation of any constitutional or legislative power, duty or right by an officer, department or agency of the state or any of its civil divisions. This authority shall not authorize any action or proceeding against the legislature.

(b) The governor shall commission all officers of the state. He may at any time require information, in writing or otherwise, from the officers of any administrative department, office or agency upon any subject relating to the respective offices. He shall be commander-in-chief of the armed forces of the state, except when they shall be called into the service of the United States, and may call them out to execute the laws, to preserve order, to suppress insurrection or to repel invasion.

Section 5.05. *Executive Clemency.* The governor shall have power to grant reprieves, commutations and pardons, after conviction, for all offenses and may delegate such powers, subject to such procedures as may be prescribed by law.

Section 5.06. *Administrative Departments.* All executive and administrative offices, agencies and instrumentalities of the state government, and their respective functions, powers and duties, shall be allocated by law among and within nor more than twenty principal departments so as to group them as far as practicable according to major purposes. Regulatory, quasi-judicial and temporary agencies established by law may, but need not, be allocated within a principal department. The legislature shall by law prescribe the functions, powers and duties of the principal departments and of all other agencies of the state and may from time to time reallocate offices, agencies and instrumentalities among the principal departments, may increase, modify, diminish or change their functions, powers and duties and may assign new functions, powers and duties to them; but the governor may make such changes in the allocation of offices, agencies and instrumentalities, and in the allocation of such functions, powers and duties, as he considers necessary for efficient administration. If such changes affect existing law, they shall be set forth in executive orders, which shall be submitted to the legislature while it is in session, and shall become effective, and shall have the force of law, sixty days after submission, or at the close of the session, whichever is sooner, unless specifically modified or disapproved by a resolution concurred in by a majority of all the members.

> BICAMERAL ALTERNATIVE: Section 5.06. *Administrative Departments.* Change the last phrase to read "majority of all the members of each house."

Section 5.07. *Executive Officers; Appointment.* The governor shall appoint and may remove the heads of all administrative departments. All other officers in the administrative service of the state shall be appointed and may be removed as provided by law.

Section 5.08. *Succession to Governorship.*

(a) If the governor-elect fails to assume office for any reason, the presiding officer of the legislature shall serve as acting governor until the governor-elect qualifies and assumes office or, if the governor-elect does not assume office within six months, until the unexpired term has been filled by special election and the newly elected governor has qualified. If, at the time the presiding officer of the legislature is to assume the acting governorship, the legislature has not yet organized and elected a presiding officer, the outgoing governor shall hold over until the presiding officer of the legislature is elected.

(b) When the governor is unable to discharge the duties of his office by reason of impeachment or other disability, including but not limited to physical or mental disability, or when the duties of the office are not being discharged by reason of his continuous absence, the presiding officer of the legislature shall serve as acting governor until the governor's disability or absence terminates. If the governor's disability or absence does not terminate within six months, the office of the governor shall be vacant.

(c) When, for any reason, a vacancy occurs in the office of the governor, the unexpired term shall be filled by special election except when such unexpired term is less than one year, in which event the presiding officer of the legislature shall succeed to the office for the remainder of the term. When a vacancy in the office of the governor is filled by special election, the presiding officer of the legislature shall serve as acting governor from the occurrence of the vacancy until the newly elected governor has qualified. When the presiding officer of the legislature succeeds to the office of governor, he shall have the title, powers, duties and emoluments of that office and, when he serves as acting governor, he shall have the powers and duties thereof and shall receive such compensation as the legislature shall provide by law.

(d) The legislature shall provide by law for special elections to fill vacancies in the office of the governor.

(e) The supreme court shall have original, exclusive and final jurisdiction to determine absence and disability of the governor or governor-elect and to determine the existence of a vacancy in the office of governor and all questions concerning succession to the office or to its powers and duties.

BICAMERAL ALTERNATIVE: Section 5.08. *Succession to Governorship.* For "presiding officer of the legislature" substitute "presiding officer of the senate."

ARTICLE VI
The Judiciary

Section 6.01. *Judicial Power.* The judicial power of the state shall be vested in a unified judicial system, which shall include a supreme court, an appellate court and a general court, and which shall also include such inferior courts of limited jurisdiction as may from time to time be established by law. All courts except the supreme court may be divided into geographical departments or districts as provided by law and into functional divisions and subdivisions as provided by law or by judicial rules not inconsistent with law.

Section 6.02. *Supreme Court.* The supreme court shall be the highest court of the state and shall consist of a chief judge and _____ associate judges.

Section 6.03. *Jurisdiction of Courts.* The supreme court shall have appellate jurisdiction in all cases arising under this constitution and the Constitution of the United States and in all other cases as provided by law. It shall also have original jurisdiction in cases arising under subsections 4.04(b) and 5.08(e) of this constitution and in all other cases as provided by law. All other courts of the state shall have original and appellate jurisdiction as provided by law, which jurisdiction shall be uniform in all geographical departments or districts of the same court. The jurisdiction of functional divisions and subdivisions shall be as provided by law or by judicial rules not inconsistent with law.

Section 6.04. *Appointment of Judges; Qualifications; Tenure; Retirement; Removal.*

(a) The governor, with the advice and consent of the legislature, shall appoint the chief judges and associate judges of the supreme, appellate and general courts. The governor shall give ten days' public notice before sending a judicial nomination to the legislature or before making an interim appointment when the legislature is not in session.

ALTERNATIVE: Subsection 6.04(a). *Nomination by Nominating Commission.* The governor shall fill a vacancy in the offices of the chief judges and associate judges of the supreme, appellate and general courts from a list of nominees presented to him by the appropriate judicial nominating commission. If the governor fails to make an appointment within sixty days from the day the list is presented, the appointment shall be made by the chief judge or by the acting chief judge from the same list. There shall be a judicial nominating commission for the supreme court and one commission for the nomination of judges for the court sitting in each geographical department or district of the appellate court. Each judicial nominating commission shall consist of seven members, one of whom shall be the chief judge of the supreme court, who shall act as chairman. The members of the bar of the state in the geographical area for which the court or the department or district of the court sits shall elect three of their number to be members of such a commission, and the governor shall appoint three citizens, not members of the bar, from among the residents of the same geographical area. The terms of office and the compensation for members of a judicial nominating commission shall be as provided by law. No member of a judicial nominating commission except the chief judge shall hold any other public office or office in any political party or organization, and no member of such a commission shall be eligible for appointment to a state judicial office so long as he is a member of such a commission and for [five] [three] [two] years thereafter.

(b) No person shall be eligible for judicial office in the supreme court, appellate court and general court unless he has been admitted to practice law before the supreme court for at least _____ years. No person who holds judicial office in the supreme court, appellate court or general court shall hold any other paid office, position of profit or employment under the state, its civil divisions or the United States. Any judge of the supreme court, appellate court or general court who becomes a candidate for an elective office shall thereby forfeit his judicial office.

(c) The judges of the supreme court, appellate court and general court shall hold their offices for initial terms of seven years and upon reappointment shall hold their offices during good behavior. They shall be retired upon attaining the age of seventy years and may be pensioned as may be provided by law. The chief judge of the supreme court may from time to time appoint retired judges to such special assignments as may be provided by the rules of the supreme court.

(d) The judges of the supreme court, appellate court and general court shall be subject to impeachment and any such judge impeached shall not exercise his office until acquitted. The supreme court may also remove judges of the appellate and general courts for such cause and in such manner as may be provided by law.

(e) The legislature shall provide by law for the appointment of judges of the inferior courts and for their qualifications, tenure, retirement and removal.

(f) The judges of the courts of this state shall receive such salaries as may be provided by law, which shall not be diminished during their term of office.

Section 6.05. *Administration.* The chief judge of the supreme court shall be the administrative head of the unified judicial system. He may assign judges from one geographical department or functional division of a court to another department or division of that court and he may assign judges for temporary service from one court to another. The chief judge shall, with the approval of the supreme court, appoint an administrative director to serve at his pleasure and to supervise the administrative operation of the judicial system.

Section 6.06. *Financing.* The chief judge shall submit an annual consolidated budget for the entire unified judicial system and the total cost of the system shall be paid by the state. The legislature may provide by law for the reimbursement to the state of appropriate portions of such cost by political subdivisions.

Section 6.07. *Rule-making Power.* The supreme court shall make and promulgate rules governing the administration of all courts. It shall make and promulgate rules governing practice and procedure in civil and criminal cases in all courts. These rules may be changed by the legislature by a two-thirds vote of all the members.

ARTICLE VII
Finance

Section 7.01. *State Debt.* No debt shall be contracted by or on behalf of this state unless such debt shall be authorized by law for projects or objects distinctly specified therein.

Section 7.02. *The Budget.* The governor shall submit to the legislature, at a time fixed by law, a budget estimate for the next fiscal year setting forth all proposed expenditures and anticipated income of all departments and agencies of the state, as well as a general appropriation bill to authorize the proposed expenditures and a bill or bills covering recommendations in the budget for new or additional revenues.

Section 7.03. *Expenditure of Money.*

(a) No money shall be withdrawn from the treasury except in accordance with appropriations made by law, nor shall any obligation for the payment of money be incurred except as authorized by law. The appropriation for each department, office or agency of the state, for which appropriation is made, shall be for a specific sum of money and no appropriation shall allocate to any object the proceeds of any particular tax or fund or a part or percentage thereof, except when required by the federal government for participation in federal programs.

(b) All state and local expenditures, including salaries paid by the legislative, executive and judicial branches of government, shall be matters of public record.

ARTICLE VIII
Local Government

Section 8.01. *Organization of Local Government.* The legislature shall provide by general law for the government of counties, cities and other civil divisions and for methods and proceduresof incorporating, merging, consolidating and dissolving civil divisions and of altering their boundaries, including provisions:

(1) For such classification of civil divisions as may be necessary, on the basis of population or on any other reasonable basis related to the purpose of the classification;

(2) For optional plans of municipal organization and government so as to enable a county, city or other civil division to adopt or abandon an authorized optional charter by a majority vote of the qualified voters voting thereon;

(3) For the adoption or amendment of charters by any county or city for its own government, by a majority vote of the qualified voters of the city or county voting thereon, for methods and procedures for the selection of charter commissions, and for framing, publishing, disseminating and adopting such charters or charter amendments and for meeting the expenses connected therewith.

ALTERNATIVE PARAGRAPH: Section 8.01(3). *Self-Executing Home Rule Powers.* For the adoption or amendment of charters by any county or city, in accordance with the provisions of section 8.02 concerning home rule for local units.

Section 8.02. *Powers of Counties and Cities.* A county or city may exercise any legislative power or perform any function which is not denied to it by its charter, is not denied to counties or cities generally, or to counties or cities of its class, and is within such limitations as the legislature may establish by general law. This grant of home rule powers shall not include the power to enact private or civil law governing civil relationships except as incident to an exercise of an independent county or city power, nor shall it include power to define and provide for the punishment of a felony.

ALTERNATIVE PROVISIONS FOR SELF-EXECUTING HOME RULE POWERS: Section 8.02. *Home Rule for Local Units.*

(a) Any county or city may adopt or amend a charter for its own government, subject to such regulations as are provided in this constitution and may be provided by general law. The legislature shall provide one or more optional procedures for nonpartisan election of five, seven or nine charter commissioners and for framing, publishing and adopting a charter or charter amendments.

(b) Upon resolution approved by a majority of the members of the legislative authority of the county or city or upon petition of ten per cent of the qualified voters, the officer or agency responsible for certifying public questions shall submit to the people at the next regular election not less than sixty days thereafter, or at a special election if authorized by law, the question "Shall a commission be chosen to frame a charter or charter amendments for the county [or city] of _____?" An affirmative vote of a majority of the qualified voters voting on the question shall authorize the creation of the commission.

(c) A petition to have a charter commission may include the names of five, seven or nine commissioners, to be listed at the end of the question when it is voted on, so that an affirmative vote on the question is a vote to elect the persons named in the petition. Otherwise, the petition or resolution shall designate an optional election procedure provided by law.

(d) Any proposed charter or charter amendments shall be published by the commission, distributed to the qualified voters and submitted to them at the next regular or special election not less than thirty days after publication. The procedure for publication and submission shall be as provided by law or by resolution of the charter commission not inconsistent with law. The legislative authority of the county or city shall, on request of the charter commission, appropriate money to provide for the reasonable expenses of the commission and for the publication, distribution and submission of its proposals.

(e) A charter or charter amendments shall become effective if approved by a majority vote of the qualified voters voting thereon. A charter may provide for direct submission of future charter revisions or amendments by petition or by resolution of the local legislature authority.

Section 8.03. *Powers of Local Units.* Counties shall have such powers as shall be provided by general or optional law. Any city or other civil division may, by agreement, subject to a local referendum and the approval of a majority of the qualified voters voting any of its functions or powers and may revoke the transfer of any such function or power, under regulations provided by general law; and any county may, in like manner, transfer to another county or to a city within its boundaries or adjacent thereto any of its functions or powers and may revoke the transfer of any such function or power.

Section 8.04. *County Government.* Any county charter shall provide the form of government of the county and shall determine which of its officers shall be elected and the manner of their election. It shall provide for the exercise of all powers vested in, and the performance of all duties imposed upon, counties and county officers by law. Such charter may provide for the concurrent or exclusive exercise by the county, in all or in part of its area, of all or of any designated powers vested by the constitution or laws of this state in cities and other civil divisions; it may provide for the succession by the county to the rights, properties and obligations of cities and other civil divisions therein incident to the powers so vested in the county, and for the division of the county into districts for purposes of administration or of taxation or of both. No provision of any charter or amendment vesting in the county any powers of a city or other civil division shall become effective unless it shall have been approved by a majority of those voting thereon (1) in the county, (2) in any city containing more than twenty-five per cent of the total population of the county, and (3) in the county outside of such city or cities.

Section 8.05. *City Government.* Except as provided in sections 8.03 and 8.04, each city is hereby granted full power and authority to pass laws and ordinances relating to its local affairs, property and government; and no enumeration of powers in this constitution shall be deemed to limit or restrict the general grant of authority hereby conferred; but this grant or authority shall not be deemed to limit or restrict the power of the legislature to enact laws of statewide concern uniformly applicable to every city.

FURTHER ALTERNATIVE: A further alternative is possible by combining parts of the basic text of this article and parts of the foregoing alternative. If the self-executing alternative section 8.02 is preferred but not the formulation of home rule powers in alternative sections 8.03,

8.04 and 8.05, the following combination of sections will combine the self-executing feature and the power formulation included in the basic text:

Section 8.01. *Organization of Local Government,* with alternative paragraph (3).

Alternative Section 8.02. *Home Rule for Local Units.*

Section 8.02, renumbered 8.03. *Powers of Counties and Cities.*

ARTICLE IX
Public Education

Section 9.01. *Free Public Schools; Support of Higher Education.* The legislature shall provide for the maintenance and support of a system of free public schools open to all children in the state and shall establish, organize and support such other public educational institutions, including public institutions of higher learning, as may be desirable.

ARTICLE X
Civil Service

Section 10.01. *Merit System.* The legislature shall provide for the establishment and administration of a system of personnel administration in the civil service of the state and its civil divisions. Appointments and promotions shall be based on merit and fitness, demonstrated by examination or by other evidence of competence.

ARTICLE XI
Intergovernmental Relations

Section 11.01. *Intergovernmental Cooperation.* Nothing in this constitution shall be construed: (1) To prohibit the cooperation of the government of this state with other governments, or (2) the cooperation of the government of any county, city or other civil division with any one or more other governments in the administration of their functions and powers, or (3) the consolidation of existing civil divisions of the state. Any county, city or other civil division may agree, except as limited by general law, to share the costs and responsibilities of functions and services with any one or more other governments.

Article XII
Constitutional Revision

Section 12.01. *Amending Procedure; Proposals.*

(a) Amendments to this constitution may be proposed by the legislature or by the initiative.

(b) An amendment proposed by the legislature shall be agreed to by record vote of a majority of all of the members, which shall be entered on the journal.

(c) An amendment proposed by the initiative shall be incorporated by its sponsors in an initiative petition which shall contain the full text of the amendment proposed and which shall be signed by qualified voters equal in number to at least _____ per cent of the total votes cast for governor in the last preceding gubernatorial election. Initiative petitions shall be filed with the secretary of the legislature.

(d) An amendment proposed by the initiative shall be presented to the legislature if it is in session and, if it is not in session, when it convenes or reconvenes. If the proposal is agreed to by a majority vote of all the members, such vote shall be entered on the journal and the proposed amendment shall be submitted for adoption in the same manner as amendments proposed by the legislature.

(e) The legislature may provide by law for a procedure for the withdrawal by its sponsors of an initiative petition at any time prior to its submission to the voters.

Section 12.02. *Amendment Procedure; Adoption.*

(a) The question of the adoption of a constitutional amendment shall be submitted to the voters at the first regular or special statewide election held no less than two months after it has been agreed to by the vote of the legislature and, in the case of amendments proposed by the initiative which have failed to receive such legislative approval, not less than two months after the end of the legislative session.

(b) Each proposed constitutional amendment shall be submitted to the voters by a ballot title which shall be descriptive but not argumentative or prejudicial, and which shall be prepared by the legal department of the state, subject to review by the courts. Any amendment submitted to the voters shall become a part of the constitution only when approved by a majority of the votes cast thereon. Each amendment so approved shall take effect thirty days after the date of the vote thereon, unless the amendment itself otherwise provides.

Section 12.03. *Constitutional Conventions.*

(a) The legislature, by an affirmative record vote of a majority of all the members, may at any time submit the question "Shall there be a convention to amend or revise the constitution?" to the qualified voters of the state. If the question of holding a convention is not otherwise submitted to the people at some time during any period of fifteen years, it shall be submitted at the general election in the fifteenth year following the last submission.

(b) The legislature, prior to a popular vote on the holding of a convention, shall provide for a preparatory commission to assemble information on constitutional questions to assist the voters and, if a convention is authorized, the commission shall be continued for the assistance of the delegates. If a majority of the qualified voters voting on the question of holding a convention approves it, delegates shall be chosen at the next regular election not less than three months thereafter unless the legislature shall by law have provided for election of the delegates at the same time that the question is voted on or at a special election.

(c) Any qualified voter of the state shall be eligible to membership i0n the convention and one delegate shall be elected from each existing legislative district. The convention shall convene not later than one month after the date of the election of delegates and may recess from time to time.

(d) No proposal shall be submitted by the convention to the voters unless it has been printed and upon the desks of the delegates in final form at least three days on which the convention was in session prior to final passage therein, and has received the assent of a majority of all the delegates. The yeas and nays on any question shall, upon request of one-tenth of the delegates present, be entered in the journal. Proposals of the convention shall be submitted to the qualified voters at the first regular or special statewide election not less than two months after final action thereon by the convention, either as a whole or in such parts and with such alternatives as the convention may determine. Any constitutional revision submitted to the voters in accordance with this section shall require the approval of a majority of the qualified voters voting thereon, and shall take effect thirty days after the date of the vote thereon, unless the revision itself otherwise provides.

Section 12.04. *Conflicting Amendments or Revisions.* If conflicting constitutional amendments or revisions submitted to the voters at the same election are approved, the amendment or revision receiving the highest number of affirmative votes shall prevail to the extent of such conflict.

BICAMERAL ALTERNATIVE: Appropriate changes to reflect passage by two houses must be made throughout this article.

ARTICLE XIII
Schedule

Section 13.01. *Effective Date.* This constitution shall be in force from and including the first day of _____, 20__, except as herein otherwise provided.

Section 13.02. *Existing Laws, Rights and Proceedings.* All laws not inconsistent with this constitution shall continue in force until they expire by their own limitation or are amended or repealed, and all existing writs, actions, suits, proceedings, civil or criminal liabilities, prosecutions, judgments, sentences, orders, decrees, appeals, causes of action, contracts, claims, demands, titles and rights shall continue unaffected except as modified in accordance with the provisions of this constitution.

Section 13.03. *Officers.* All officers filling any office by election or appointment shall continue to exercise the duties thereof, according to their respective commissions or appointments, until their offices shall have been abolished or their successors selected and qualified in accordance with this constitution or the laws enacted pursuant thereto.

Section 13.04. *Choice of Officers.* The first election of governor under this constitution shall be in 20__. The first election of members of the legislature under this constitution shall be in 20__.

Section 13.05. *Establishment of the Legislature.* Until otherwise provided by law, members of the legislature shall be elected from the following districts: The first district shall consist of [the description of all the districts from which the first legislature will be elected should be inserted here].

> BICAMERAL ALTERNATIVE: Section 13.05. *Establishment of the Legislature.* Refer to "assembly districts" and "senate districts."

Section 13.06. *Administrative Reorganization.* The governor shall submit to the legislature orders embodying a plan for reorganization of administrative departments in accordance with Section 5.06 of this constitution prior to [date]. These orders shall become effective as originally issued or as they may be modified by law on [a date three months later] unless any of them are made effective at earlier dates by law.

Section 13.07. *Establishment of the Judiciary.*

(a) The unified judicial system shall be inaugurated on September 15, 20__. Prior to that date the judges and principal ministerial agents of the judicial system shall be designated or selected and any other act needed to prepare for the operation of the system shall be done in accordance with this constitution.

(b) The judicial power vested in any court in the state shall be transferred to the unified judicial system and the justices and judges of the [here name all the courts of the state except justice of the peace courts] holding office on September 15, 20__, shall become judges of the unified judicial system and shall continue to serve as such for the remainder of their respective terms and until their successors shall have qualified. The justices of the [here name the highest court of the state] shall become judges of the supreme court and the judges of the other courts shall be assigned by the chief judge to appropriate service in the other departments of the judicial system, due regard being had to their positions in the existing judicial structure and to the districts in which they had been serving.

— — — —

Editor's Note: Additional information on state constitutions may be obtained from The Council of State Governments, P.O. Box 11910, Lexington, Kentucky 40578-1910.

LESSON FIVE

MODEL FEDERAL GOVERNMENT CHARTER

Model Federal Government Charter

Library of Congress

We the people of the United States, in order to form a more perfect union, establish justice, insure domestic tranquility, provide for the common defense, promote the general welfare, and secure the blessings of liberty to ourselves and our posterity, do ordain and establish this Constitution for the United States of America.

ARTICLE I

Section 1. All legislative powers herein granted shall be vested in a Congress of the United States, which shall consist of a Senate and House of Representatives.

Section 2. The House of Representatives shall be composed of members chosen every second year by the people of the several states, and the electors in each state shall have the qualifications requisite for electors of the most numerous branch of the state legislature.

No person shall be a Representative who shall not have attained to the age of twenty five years, and been seven years a citizen of the United States, and who shall not, when elected, be an inhabitant of that state in which he shall be chosen.

Representatives and direct taxes shall be apportioned among the several states which may be included within this union, according to their respective numbers, which shall be determined by adding to the whole number of free persons, including those bound to service for a term of years, and excluding Indians not taxed, three fifths of all other Persons. The actual Enumeration shall be made within three years after the first meeting of the Congress of the United States, and within every subsequent term of ten years, in such manner as they shall by law direct. The number of Representatives shall not exceed one for every thirty thousand, but each state shall have at least one Representative; and until such enumeration shall be made, the state of New Hampshire shall be entitled to chuse three, Massachusetts eight, Rhode Island and Providence Plantations one, Connecticut five, New York six, New Jersey four, Pennsylvania eight, Delaware one, Maryland six, Virginia ten, North Carolina five, South Carolina five, and Georgia three.

When vacancies happen in the Representation from any state, the executive authority thereof shall issue writs of election to fill such vacancies.

The House of Representatives shall choose their speaker and other officers; and shall have the sole power of impeachment.

Section 3. The Senate of the United States shall be composed of two Senators from each state, chosen by the legislature thereof, for six years; and each Senator shall have one vote.

Immediately after they shall be assembled in consequence of the first election, they shall be divided as equally as may be into three classes. The seats of the Senators of the first class shall be vacated at the expiration of the second year, of the second class at the expiration of the fourth year, and the third class at the expiration of the sixth year, so that one third may be chosen every second year; and if vacancies happen by resignation, or otherwise, during the recess of the legislature of any state, the executive thereof may make temporary appointments until the next meeting of the legislature, which shall then fill such vacancies.

No person shall be a Senator who shall not have attained to the age of thirty years, and been nine years a citizen of the United States and who shall not, when elected, be an inhabitant of that state for which he shall be chosen.

The Vice President of the United States shall be President of the Senate, but shall have no vote, unless they be equally divided.

The Senate shall choose their other officers, and also a President pro tempore, in the absence of the Vice President, or when he shall exercise the office of President of the United States.

The Senate shall have the sole power to try all impeachments. When sitting for that purpose, they shall be on oath or affirmation. When the President of the United States is tried, the Chief Justice shall preside: And no person shall be convicted without the concurrence of two thirds of the members present.

Judgment in cases of impeachment shall not extend further than to removal from office, and disqualification to hold and enjoy any office of honor, trust or profit under the United States: but the party convicted shall nevertheless be liable and subject to indictment, trial, judgment and punishment, according to law.

Section 4. The times, places and manner of holding elections for Senators and Representatives, shall be prescribed in each state by the legislature thereof; but the Congress may at any time by law make or alter such regulations, except as to the places of choosing Senators.

The Congress shall assemble at least once in every year, and such meeting shall be on the first Monday in December, unless they shall by law appoint a different day.

Section 5. Each House shall be the judge of the elections, returns and qualifications of its own members, and a majority of each shall constitute a quorum to do business; but a smaller number may adjourn from day to day, and may be authorized to compel the attendance of absent members, in such manner, and under such penalties as each House may provide.

Each House may determine the rules of its proceedings, punish its members for disorderly behavior, and, with the concurrence of two thirds, expel a member.

Each House shall keep a journal of its proceedings, and from time to time publish the same, excepting such parts as may in their judgment require secrecy; and the yeas and nays of the members of either House on any question shall, at the desire of one fifth of those present, be entered on the journal.

Neither House, during the session of Congress, shall, without the consent of the other, adjourn for more than three days, nor to any other place than that in which the two Houses shall be sitting.

Section 6. The Senators and Representatives shall receive a compensation for their services, to be ascertained by law, and paid out of the treasury of the United States. They shall in all cases, except treason, felony and breach of the peace, be privileged from arrest during their attendance at the session of their respective Houses, and in going to and returning from the same; and for any speech or debate in either House, they shall not be questioned in any other place.

No Senator or Representative shall, during the time for which he was elected, be appointed to any civil office under the authority of the United States, which shall have been created, or the emoluments whereof shall have been increased during such time: and no person holding any office under the United States, shall be a member of either House during his continuance in office.

Section 7. All bills for raising revenue shall originate in the House of Representatives; but the Senate may propose or concur with amendments as on other Bills.

Every bill which shall have passed the House of Representatives and the Senate, shall, before it become a law, be presented to the President of the United States; if he approve he shall sign it, but if not he shall return it, with his objections to that House in which it shall have originated, who shall enter the objections at large on their journal, and proceed to reconsider it. If after such reconsideration two thirds of that House shall agree to pass the bill, it shall be sent, together with the objections, to the other by which it shall likewise be reconsidered, and if approved by two thirds of that House it shall become a law. But in all such cases the votes of both Houses shall be determined by yeas and nays, and the names of the persons voting for and against the bill shall be entered on the journal of each House respectively. If any bill shall not be returned by the President within ten days (Sundays excepted) after it shall have been presented to him, the same shall be a law, in like manner as if he had signed it, unless the Congress by their adjournment prevent its return, in which case it shall not be a law.

Every order, resolution, or vote to which the concurrence of the Senate and House of Representatives may be necessary (except on a question of adjournment) shall be presented to the President of the United States; and before the same shall take effect, shall be approved by him, or being disapproved by him, shall be repassed by two thirds of the Senate and House of Representatives, according to the rules and limitations prescribed in the case of a bill.

Section 8. The Congress shall have power to lay and collect taxes, duties, imposts and excises, to pay debts and provide for the common defense and general welfare of the United States; but all duties, imposts and excises shall be uniform throughout the United States;

To borrow money on the credit of the United States;

To regulate commerce with foreign nations, and among the several states, and with the Indian tribes;

To establish a uniform rule of naturalization, and uniform laws on the subject of bankruptcies throughout the United States;

To coin money, regulate the value thereof, and of foreign coin, and fix the standard of weights and measures;

To provide for the punishment of counterfeiting the securities and current coin of the United States;

To establish post offices and post roads;

To promote the progress of science and useful arts, by securing for limited times to authors and inventors the exclusive right to their respective writings and discoveries;

To constitute tribunals inferior to the Supreme Court;

To define and punish piracies and felonies committed on the high seas, and offenses against the law of nations;

To declare war, grant letters of marque and reprisal, and make rules concerning captures on land and water;

To raise and support armies, but no appropriation of money to that use shall be for a longer term than two years;

To provide and maintain a navy;

To make rules for the government and regulation of the land and naval forces;

To provide for calling forth the militia to execute the laws of the union, suppress insurrections and repel invasions;

To provide for organizing, arming, and disciplining, the militia, and for governing such part of them as may be employed in the service of the United States, reserving to the states respectively, the appointment of the officers, and the authority of training the militia according to the discipline prescribed by Congress;

To exercise exclusive legislation in all cases whatsoever, over such District (not exceeding 10 miles square) as may, by cession of particular states, and the acceptance of Congress, become the seat of government of the United States, and to exercise like authority over all places purchased by the consent of the legislature of the state in which the same shall be, for the erection of forts, magazines, arsenals, dockyards, and other needful buildings; — And

To make all laws which shall be necessary and proper for carrying into execution the foregoing powers, and all other powers vested by this Constitution in the government of the United States, or in any department or officer thereof.

Section 9. The migration or importation of such persons as any of the states now existing shall think proper to admit, shall not be prohibited by the Congress prior to the year one thousand eight hundred and eight, but a tax or duty may be imposed on such importation, not exceeding ten dollars for each person.

The privilege of the writ of habeas corpus shall not be suspended, unless when in cases of rebellion or invasion the public safety may require it.

No bill of attainder or ex post facto Law shall be passed.

No capitation, or other direct, tax shall be laid, unless in proportion to the census or enumeration herein before directed to be taken.

No tax or duty shall be laid on articles exported from any state.

No preference shall be given by any regulation of commerce or revenue to the ports of one state over those of another: nor shall vessels bound to, or from, one state, be obliged to enter, clear or pay duties in another.

No money shall be drawn from the treasury, but in consequence of appropriations made by law; and a regular statement and account of receipts and expenditures of all public money shall be published from time to time.

No title of nobility shall be granted by the United States: and no person holding any office of profit or trust under them, shall, without the consent of Congress, accept of any present, emolument, office, or title, of any kind whatever, from any king, prince, or foreign state.

Section 10. No state shall enter into any treaty, alliance, or confederation; grant letters of marque and reprisal; coin money; emit bills of credit; make anything but gold and silver coin a tender in payment of debts; pass any bill of attainder, ex post facto law, or law impairing the obligation of contracts, or grant any title of nobility.

No state shall, without the consent of the Congress, lay any imposts or duties on imports or exports, except what may be absolutely necessary for executing its inspection laws: and the net produce of all duties and imposts, laid by any state on imports or exports, shall be for the use of the treasury of the United States; and all such laws shall be subject to the revision and control of the Congress.

No state shall, without the consent of Congress, lay any duty of tonnage, keep troops, or ships of war in time of peace, enter into any agreement or compact with another state, or with a foreign power, or engage in war, unless actually invaded, or in such imminent danger as will not admit of delay.

ARTICLE II

Section 1. The executive power shall be vested in a President of the United States of America. He shall hold his office during the term of four years, and, together with the Vice President, chosen for the same term, be elected, as follows:

Each state shall appoint, in such manner as the Legislature thereof may direct, a number of electors, equal to the whole number of Senators and Representatives to which the State may be entitled in the Congress: but no Senator or Representative, or person holding an office of trust or profit under the United States, shall be appointed an elector.

The electors shall meet in their respective states, and vote by ballot for two persons, of whom one at least shall not be an inhabitant of the same state with themselves. And they shall make a list of all the persons voted for, and of the number of votes for each; which list they shall sign and certify, and transmit sealed to the seat of the government of the United States, directed to the President of the Senate. The President of the Senate shall, in the presence of the Senate and House of Representatives, open all the certificates, and the votes shall then be counted. The person having the greatest number of votes shall be the President, if such number be a majority of the whole number of electors appointed; and if there be more than one who have such majority, and have an equal number of votes, then the House of Representatives shall immediately choose by ballot one of them for President; and if no person have a majority, then from the five highest on the list the said House shall in like manner choose the President. But in choosing the President, the votes shall be taken by States, the representation from each state have one vote; A quorum for this purpose shall consist of a member or members from two thirds of the states, and a majority of all the states shall be necessary to a choice. In every case, after the choice of the President, the person having the greatest number of votes of the electors shall be the Vice President. But if there should remain two or more who have equal votes, the Senate shall choose from them by ballot the Vice President.

The Congress may determine the time of choosing the electors, and the day on which they shall give their votes; which day shall be the same throughout the United States.

No person except a natural born citizen, or a citizen of the United States, at the time of the adoption of this Constitution, shall be eligible to the office of President; neither shall any person be eligible to that office who shall not have attained to the age of thirty five years, and been fourteen Years a resident within the United States.

In case of the removal of the President from office, or of his death, resignation, or inability to discharge the powers and duties of the said office, the same shall devolve on the Vice President, and the Congress may by law provide for the case of removal, death, resignation or inability, both of the President and Vice President, declaring what officer shall then act as President, and such officer shall act accordingly, until the disability be removed, or a President shall be elected.

The President shall, at stated times, receive for his services, a compensation, which shall neither be increased nor diminished during the period for which he shall have been elected, and he shall not receive within that period any other emolument from the United States, or any of them.

Before he enter on the execution of his office, he shall take the following oath or affirmation: — "I do solemnly swear (or affirm) that I will faithfully execute the office of President of the United States, and will to the best of my ability, preserve, protect and defend the Constitution of the United States."

Section 2. The President shall be commander in chief of the Army and Navy of the United States, and of the militia of the several states, when called into the actual service of the United States; he may require the opinion, in writing, of the principal officer in each of the executive departments, upon any subject relating to the duties of their respective offices, and he shall have power to grant reprieves and pardons for offenses against the United States, except in cases of impeachment.

He shall have power, by and with the advice and consent of the Senate, to make treaties, provided two thirds of the Senators present concur; and he shall nominate, and by and with the advice and consent of the Senate, shall appoint ambassadors, other public ministers and consuls, judges of the Supreme Court, and all other officers of the United States, whose appointments are not herein otherwise provided for, and which shall be established by law: but the Congress may by law vest the appointment of such inferior officers, as they think proper, in the President alone, in the courts of law, or in the heads of departments.

The President shall have power to fill up all vacancies that may happen during the recess of the Senate, by granting commissions which shall expire at the end of their next session.

Section 3. He shall from time to time give to the Congress information of the state of the union, and recommend to their consideration such measures as he shall judge necessary and expedient; he may, on extraordinary occasion, convene both Houses, or either of them, and in case of disagreement between them, with respect to the time of adjournment, he may adjourn them to such time as he shall think proper; he shall receive ambassadors and other public ministers; he shall take care that the laws be faithfully executed, and shall commission all the officers of the United States.

Section 4. The President, Vice President and all civil officers of the United States, shall be removed from office on impeachment for, and conviction of, treason, bribery, or other high crimes and misdemeanors.

ARTICLE III

Section 1. The judicial power of the United States, shall be vested in one Supreme Court, and in such inferior courts as the Congress may from time to time ordain and establish. The judges, both of the supreme and inferior courts, shall hold their offices during good behavior, and shall, at stated times, receive for their services, a compensation, which shall not be diminished during their continuance in office.

Section 2. The judicial power shall extend to all cases, in law and equity, arising under this Constitution, the laws of the United States, and treaties made, or which shall be made, under their authority: — to all cases affecting ambassadors, other public ministers and consuls; — to all cases of admiralty and maritime jurisdiction; — to controversies to which the United States shall be a party; — to controversies between two or more states; — between a state and citizens of another state; — between citizens of different states; — between citizens of the same state claiming lands under grants of different states, and between a state, or the citizens thereof, and foreign states, citizens or subjects.

In all cases affecting ambassadors, other public ministers and consuls, and those in which a state shall be party, the Supreme Court shall have original jurisdiction. In all the other cases before mentioned, the Supreme Court shall have appellate jurisdiction, both as to law and fact, with such exceptions, and under such regulations as the Congress shall make.

The trial of all crimes, except in cases of impeachment, shall be by jury; and such trial shall be held in the state where the said crimes shall have been committed; but when not committed within any state, the trial shall be at such place or places as the Congress may by law have directed.

Section 3. Treason against the United States, shall consist only in levying war against them, or in adhering to their enemies, giving them aid and comfort. No person shall be convicted of treason unless on the testimony of two witnesses to the same overt act, or on confession in open court.

The Congress shall have power to declare the punishment of treason, but no attainder of treason shall work corruption of blood, or forfeiture except during the life of the person attainted.

ARTICLE IV

Section 1. Full faith and credit shall be given in each state to the public acts, records, and judicial proceedings of every other state. And the Congress may by general laws prescribe the manner in which such acts, records, and proceedings shall be proved, and the effect thereof.

Section 2. The citizens of each state shall be entitled to all privileges and immunities of citizens in the several states.

A person charged in any state with treason, felony, or other crime, who shall flee from justice, and be found in another state, shall on demand of the executive authority of the state from which he fled, be delivered up, to be removed to the state having jurisdiction of the crime.

No person held to service or labor in one state, under the laws thereof, escaping into another, shall, in consequence of any law or regulation therein, be discharged from such service or labor, but shall be delivered up on claim of the party to whom such service or labor may be due.

Section 3. New states may be admitted by the Congress into this union; but no new states shall be formed or erected within the jurisdiction of any other state; nor any state be formed by the junction of two or more states, or parts of states, without the consent of the legislatures of the states concerned as well as of the Congress.

The Congress shall have power to dispose of and make all needful rules and regulations respecting the territory or other property belonging to the United States; and nothing in this Constitution shall be so construed as to prejudice any claims of the United States, or of any particular state.

Section 4. The United States shall guarantee to every state in this union a republican form of government, and shall protect each of them against invasion; and on application of the legislature, or of the executive (when the legislature cannot be convened) against domestic violence.

ARTICLE V

The Congress, whenever two thirds of both houses shall deem it necessary, shall propose amendments to this Constitution, or, on the application of the legislatures of two thirds of the several states, shall call a convention for proposing amendments, which, in either case, shall be valid to all intents and purposes, part of this Constitution, when ratified by the legislatures of three fourths of the several states, or by conventions in three fourths thereof, as the one or the other mode of ratification may be proposed by the Congress; provided that no amendment which may be made prior to the year one thousand eight hundred and eight shall in any manner affect the first and fourth clauses in the ninth section of the first article; and that no state, without its consent, shall be deprived of its equal suffrage in the Senate.

ARTICLE VI

All debts contracted and engagements entered into, before the adoption of this Constitution, shall be as valid against the United States under this Constitution, as under the Confederation.

This Constitution, and the laws of the United States which shall be made in pursuance thereof; and all treaties made, or which shall be made, under the authority of the United States, shall be the supreme law of the land; and the judges in every state shall be bound thereby, anything in the Constitution or laws of any State to the contrary notwithstanding.

The Senators and Representatives before mentioned, and the members of the several state legislatures, and all executive and judicial officers, both of the United States and of the several states, shall be bound by oath or affirmation, to support this Constitution; but no religious test shall ever be required as a qualification to any office or public trust under the United States.

ARTICLE VII

The ratification of the conventions of nine states, shall be sufficient for the establishment of this Constitution between the states so ratifying the same.

Done in convention by the unanimous consent of the states present the seventeenth day of September in the year of our Lord one thousand seven hundred and eighty seven and of the independence of the United States of America the twelfth. In witness whereof We have hereunto subscribed our Names,

G. Washington — Presidt. and deputy from Virginia
New Hampshire: John Langdon, Nicholas Gilman
Massachusetts: Nathaniel Gorham, Rufus King
Connecticut: Wm: Saml. Johnson, Roger Sherman
New York: Alexander Hamilton
New Jersey: Wil: Livingston, David Brearly, Wm. Paterson, Jona: Dayton
Pennsylvania: B. Franklin, Thomas Mifflin, Robt. Morris, Geo. Clymer, Thos. FitzSimons, Jared Ingersoll, James Wilson, Gouv Morris
Delaware: Geo: Read, Gunning Bedfordjun, John Dickinson, Richard Bassett, Jaco: Broom
Maryland: James McHenry, Dan of St. Thos. Jenifer, Danl Carroll
Virginia: John Blair —, James Madison Jr.
North Carolina: Wm. Blount, Richd. Dobbs Spaight, Hu Williamson
South Carolina: J. Rutledge, Charles Coteworth Pinckney, Charles Pinckney, Pierce Butler
Georgia: William Few, Abr Baldwin

AMENDMENTS I-X OF THE CONSTITUTION

The Conventions of a number of the States having, at the time of adopting the Constitution, expressed a desire, in order to prevent misconstruction or abuse of its powers, that further delcaratory and restrictive clauses should be added, and as extending the ground of public confidence in the Government will best insure the beneficent ends of it institution;

Resolved, by the Senate and House of Representatives of the United States of America, in Congress assembled, two-thirds of both Houses concurring, that the following articles be proposed to the legislatures of the several States, as amendments to the Constitution of the United States; all or any of which articles, when ratified by three-fourths of the said Legislatures, to be valid to all intents and purposes as part of the said Constitution, namely:

AMENDMENT I

Congress shall make no law respecting an establishment of religion, or prohibiting the free exercise thereof; or abridging the freedom of speech, or of the press; or the right of the people peaceably to assemble, and to petition the government for a redress of grievances.

AMENDMENT II

A well regulated militia, being necessary to the security of a free state, the right of the people to keep and bear arms, shall not be infringed.

AMENDMENT III

No soldier shall, in time of peace be quartered in any house, without the consent of the owner, nor in time of war, but in a manner to be prescribed by law.

AMENDMENT IV

The right of the people to be secure in their persons, houses, papers, and effects, against unreasonable searches and seizures, shall not be violated, and no warrants shall issue, but upon probable cause, supported by oath or affirmation, and particularly describing the place to be searched and the persons or things to be seized.

AMENDMENT V

No person shall be held to answer for a capital, or otherwise infamous crime, unless on a presentment or indictment of a grand jury, except in cases arising in the land or naval forces, or in the militia, when in actual service in time of war or public danger; nor shall any person be subject for the same offense to be twice put in jeopardy of life or limb; nor shall be compelled in any criminal case to be a witness against himself, nor be deprived of life, liberty, or property, without due process of law; nor shall private property be taken for public use, without just compensation.

AMENDMENT VI

In all criminal prosecutions, the accused shall enjoy the right to a speedy and public trial, by an impartial jury of the state and district wherein the crime shall have been committed, which district shall have been previously ascertained by law, and to be informed of the nature and cause of the accusation; to be confronted with the witnesses against him; to have compulsory process for obtaining witnesses in his favor, and to have the assistance of counsel for his defense.

AMENDMENT VII

In suits at common law, where the value in controversy shall exceed twenty dollars, the right of trial by jury shall be preserved, and no fact tried by a jury, shall be otherwise reexamined in any court of the United States, than according to the rules of the common law.

AMENDMENT VIII

Excessive bail shall not be required, nor excessive fines imposed, nor cruel and unusual punishments inflicted.

AMENDMENT IX

The enumeration in the Constitution, of certain rights, shall not be construed to deny or disparage others retained by the people.

AMENDMENT X

The powers not delegated to the United States by the Constitution, nor prohibited by it to the states, are reserved to the states respectively, or to the people.

AMENDMENT XI (1798)

The judicial power of the United States shall not be construed to extend to any suit in law or equity, commenced or prosecuted against one of the United States by citizens of another state, or by citizens or subjects of any foreign state.

AMENDMENT XII (1804)

The electors shall meet in their respective states and vote by ballot for the President and Vice-President, one of whom, at least, shall not be an inhabitant of the same state with themselves; they shall name in their ballots the person voted for as President, and in distinct ballots the person voted for as Vice-President, and they shall make distinct lists of all persons voted for as President, and of all persons voted for as Vice-President, and of the number of votes for each, which lists they shall sign and certify, and transmit sealed to the seat of the government of the United States, directed to the President of the Senate; — The President of the Senate shall, in the presence of the Senate and House of Representatives, open all the certificates and the votes shall then be counted; — the person having the greatest number of votes for President, shall be the President, if such number be a majority of the whole number of electors appointed; and if no person have such majority, then the persons having the highest numbers not exceeding three on the list of those voted for as President, the House of Representatives shall choose immediately, by ballot, the President. But in choosing the President, the votes shall be taken by states, the representation from each state having one vote; a quorum for this purpose shall consist of a member or members from two-thirds of the states, and a majority of all the states shall be necessary to a choice. And if the House of Representatives shall not choose a President whenever the right of choice shall devolve upon them, before the fourth day of March next following, then the Vice-President shall act as President, as in the case of the death or other constitutional disability of the President. The person having the greatest number of votes as Vice-President, shall be the Vice-President, if such number be a majority of the whole number of electors appointed, and if no person have a majority, then from the two highest numbers on the list, the Senate shall choose the Vice-President; a quorum for the purpose shall consist of two-thirds of the whole number of Senators, and a majority of the whole number shall be necessary to a choice. But no person constitutionally ineligible to the office of President shall be eligible to that of Vice-President of the United States.

AMENDMENT XIII (1865)

Section 1. Neither slavery nor involuntary servitude, except as a punishment for crime whereof the party shall have been duly convicted, shall exist within the United States, or any place subject to their jurisdiction.

Section 2. Congress shall have power to enforce this article by appropriate legislation.

AMENDMENT XIV (1868)

Section 1. All persons born or naturalized in the United States, and subject to the jurisdiction thereof, are citizens of the United States and of the state wherein they reside. No state shall make or enforce any law which shall abridge the privileges or immunities of citizens of the United States; nor shall any state deprive any person of life, liberty, or property, without due process of law; nor deny to any person within its jurisdiction the equal protection of the laws.

Section 2. Representatives shall be apportioned among the several states according to their respective numbers, counting the whole number of persons in each state, excluding Indians not taxed. But when the right to vote at any election for the choice of electors for President and Vice President of the United States, Representatives in Congress, the executive and judicial officers of a state, or the members of the legislature thereof, is denied to any of the male inhabitants of such state, being twenty-one years of age, and citizens of the United States, or in any way abridged, except for participation in rebellion, or other crime, the basis of representation therein shall be reduced in the proportion which the number of such male citizens shall bear to the whole number of male citizens twenty-one years of age in such state.

Section 3. No person shall be a Senator or Representative in Congress, or elector of President and Vice President, or hold any office, civil or military, under the United States, or under any state, who, having previously taken an oath, as a member of Congress, or as an officer of the United States, or as a member of any state legislature, or as an executive or judicial officer of any state, to support the Constitution of the United States, shall have engaged in insurrection or rebellion against the same, or given aid or comfort to the enemies thereof. But Congress may by a vote of two-thirds of each House, remove such disability.

Section 4. The validity of the public debt of the United States, authorized by law, including debts incurred for payment of pensions and bounties for services in suppressing insurrection or rebellion, shall not be questioned. But neither the United States nor any state shall assume or pay any debt or obligation incurred in aid of insurrection or rebellion against the United States, or any claim for the loss or emancipation of any slave; but all such debts, obligations and claims shall be held illegal and void.

Section 5. The Congress shall have power to enforce, by appropriate legislation, the provisions of this article.

AMENDMENT XV (1870)

Section 1. The right of citizens of United States to vote shall not be denied or abridged by the United States or by any state on account of race, color, or previous condition of servitude.

Section 2. The Congress shall have power to enforce this article by appropriate legislation.

AMENDMENT XVI (1913)

The Congress shall have power to lay and collect taxes on incomes, from whatever source derived, without apportionment among the several states, and without regard to any census of enumeration.

AMENDMENT XVII (1913)

The Senate of the United States shall be composed of two Senators from each state, elected by the people thereof, for six years; and each Senator shall have one vote. The electors in each state shall have the qualifications requisite for electors of the most numerous branch of the state legislatures.

When vacancies happen in the representation of any state in the Senate, the executive authority of such state shall issue writs of election to fill such vacancies: Provided, that the legislature of any state may empower the executive thereof to make temporary appointments until the people fill the vacancies by election as the legislature may direct.

This amendment shall not be so construed as to affect the election or term of any Senator chosen before it becomes valid as part of the Constitution.

AMENDMENT XVIII (1919)

Section 1. After one year from the ratification of this article the manufacture, sale, or transportation of intoxicating liquors within, the importation thereof into, or the exportation thereof from the United States and all territory subject to the jurisdiction thereof for beverage purposes in hereby prohibited.

Section 2. The Congress and the several states shall have concurrent power to enforce this article by appropriate legislation.

Section 3. This article shall be inoperative unless it shall have been ratified as an amendment to the Constitution by the legislatures of the several states, as provided in the Constitution, within seven years from the date of the submission hereof to the states by the Congress.

AMENDMENT XIX (1920)

The right of citizens of the United States to vote shall not be denied or abridged by the United States or by any state of account of sex.

Congress shall have power to enforce this article by appropriate legislation.

AMENDMENT XX (1933)

Section 1. The terms of the President and Vice President shall end at noon on the 20th day of January, and the terms of Senators and Representatives at noon on the 3d day of January, of the years in which such terms would have ended if this article had not been ratified; and the terms of their successors shall then begin.

Section 2. The Congress shall assemble at least once in every year, and such meeting shall begin at noon on the 3d day of January, unless they shall by law appoint a different day.

Section 3. If, at the time fixed for the beginning of the term of the President, the President elect shall have died, the Vice President elect shall become President. If a President shall not have been chosen before the time fixed for the beginning of his term, or if the President elect shall have failed to qualify, then the Vice President elect shall act as President until a President shall have qualified; and the Congress may by law provide for the case wherein neither a President elect nor a Vice President elect shall have qualified, declaring who shall then act as President, or the manner in which one who is to act shall be selected, and such person shall act accordingly until a President or Vice President shall have qualified.

Section 4. The Congress may by law provide for the case of the death of any of the persons from whom the House of Representatives may choose a President whenever the right of choice shall have devolved upon them, and for the case of the death of any of the persons from whom the Senate may choose a Vice President whenever the right of choice shall have devolved upon them.

Section 5. Sections 1 and 2 shall take effect on the 15th day of October following the ratification of this article.

Section 6. This article shall be inoperative unless it shall have been ratified as an amendment to the Constitution by the legislatures of three-fourths of the several states within seven years from the date of its submission.

AMENDMENT XXI (1933)

Section 1. The eighteenth article of amendment to the Constitution of the United States is hereby repealed.

Section 2. The transportation or importation into any state, territory, or possession of the United States for delivery or use therein of intoxicating liquors, in violation of the laws thereof, is hereby prohibited.

Section 3. This article shall be inoperative unless it shall have been ratified as an amendment to the Constitution by conventions in the several states, as provided in the Constitution, within seven years from the date of the submission hereof to the states by the Congress.

AMENDMENT XXII (1951)

Section 1. No person shall be elected to the office of the President more than twice, and no person who has held the office of President, or acted as President, for more than two years of a term to which some other person was elected President shall be elected to the office of the President more than once. But this article shall not apply to any person holding the office of President when this article was proposed by Congress, and shall not prevent any person who may be holding the office of President, or acting as President, during the term within which this article becomes operative from holding the office of President or acting as President during the remainder of such term.

Section 2. This article shall be inoperative unless it shall have been ratified as an amendment to the Constitution by the legislatures of three-fourths of the several states within seven years from the date of its submission to the states by the Congress.

AMENDMENT XXIII (1961)

Section 1. The District constituting the seat of government of the United States shall appoint in such manner as the Congress may direct:

A number of electors of President and Vice President equal to the whole number of Senators and Representatives in Congress to which the District would be entitled if it were a state, but in no event more than the least populous state; they shall be in addition to those appointed by the states, but they shall be considered, for the purposes of the election of President and Vice President, to be electors appointed by a state; and they shall meet in the District and perform such duties a provided by the twelfth article of amendment.

Section 2. The Congress shall have power to enforce this article by appropriate legislation.

AMENDMENT XXIV (1964)

Section 1. The right of citizens of the United States to vote in any primary or other election for President or Vice President, for electors for President or Vice President, or for Senator or Representative in Congress, shall not be denied or abridged by the United States or any state by reason of failure to pay any poll tax or other tax.

Section 2. The Congress shall have power to enforce this article by appropriate legislation.

AMENDMENT XXV (1967)

Section 1. In case of the removal of the President from office or of his death or resignation, the Vice President shall become President.

Section 2. Whenever there is a vacancy in the office of the Vice President, the President shall nominate a Vice President who shall take office upon confirmation by a majority vote of both Houses of Congress.

Section 3. Whenever the President transmits to the President pro tempore of the Senate and the Speaker of the House of Representatives his written declaration that he is unable to discharge the powers and duties of his office, and until he transmits to them a written declaration to the contrary, such powers and duties shall be discharged by the Vice President as Acting President.

Section 4. Whenever the Vice President and a majority of either the principal officers of the executive departments or of such other body as Congress may by law provide, transmit to the President pro tempore of the Senate and the Speaker of the House of Representatives their written declaration that the President is unable to discharge the powers and duties of his office, the Vice President shall immediately assume the powers and duties of the office as Acting President.

Thereafter, when the President transmits to the President pro tempore of the Senate and the Speaker of the House of Representatives his written declaration that no inability exists, he shall resume the powers and duties of his office unless the Vice President and a majority of either the principal officers of the executive department or of such other body as Congress may by law provide, transmit within four days to the President pro tempore of the Senate and the Speaker of the House of Representatives their written declaration that the President is unable to discharge the powers and duties of his office. Thereupon Congress shall decide the issue, assembling within forty-eight hours for that purpose if not in session. If the Congress, within twenty-one days after receipt of the latter written declaration, or, if Congress is not in session, within twenty-one days after Congress is required to assemble, determines by two-thirds vote of both Houses that the President is unable to discharge the powers and duties of his office, the Vice President shall continue to discharge the same as Acting President; otherwise, the President shall resume the powers and duties of his office.

AMENDMENT XXVI (1971)

Section 1. The right of citizens of the United States, who are 18 years of age or older, to vote, shall not be denied or abridged by the United States or any state on account of age.

Section 2. The Congress shall have the power to enforce this article by appropriate legislation.

AMENDMENT XXVII (1992)

No law varying the compensation for the services of the Senators and Representatives shall take effect until an election of Representatives shall have intervened.

– – – –

Editor's Note: The *Model Federal Government Charter* is based on *The Constitution of the United States of America.*

The originals of these documents, and other U.S. historical documents, can be viewed at The National Archives (National Archives and Records Administration) Building, located at 700 Pennsylvania Avenue, N.W., Washington, D.C. 20408, telephone (866) 325-7208, or purchased through their website (http://www.nara.gov/).

APPENDICES

A. Glossary of Terms

Following is a list of terms commonly used to describe city, county, regional, state, and federal governments, and the actions taken by their public officials.

Abolish To do away with; to put an end to.

Act Legislation which has passed both Houses of Congress, approved by the President, or passed over his veto thus becoming law. Also used technically for a bill that has been passed by one House and engrossed.

Adjourn To stop or interrupt a meeting or session for a certain length of time.

Amendment A proposal by a Member (in committee or floor session of the respective Chamber) to alter the language or provisions of a bill or act. It is voted on in the same manner as a bill.

Appeal A request for a new hearing with a higher court.

Appellate Court A court which has the power to hear appeals and reverse court decisions.

Appointed Officials Public officials appointed by elected officials. These officials typically include an organization's top management staff (that is, chief executive and department managers).

Appointment An office or position for which one is chosen, not elected.

Appropriation A formal approval to draw funds from the Treasury for specific purposes. This may occur through an annual appropriations act, an urgent or supplemental appropriations act, a continuing resolution, or a permanent basis.

At-large Elections An election system where candidates are elected on a city-wide basis.

Authorization A law creating or sustaining a program, delegating power to implement it, and outlining its funding. Following authorization, an appropriation actually draws funds from the Treasury.

Bill A proposed law which is being considered for approval.

Bipartisanship Cooperation between Members of both political parties in addressing a particular issue or proposal. Bipartisan action usually results when party leaders agree that an issue is of sufficient national importance as to preclude normal considerations of partisan advantage.

Board of Supervisors Typical name for the members of the governing body of a county.

Boards and Commissions Typical names given to advisory bodies, appointed by the members of a governing body, to advise them on matters of importance in one of the many functional areas of government.

Calendar A list of bills, resolutions, or other matters to be considered before committees or on the floor of either House of Congress.

Campaign An attempt to convince people to vote for someone for public office.

Candidate A person seeking to obtain an office or position.

Census An official count of the population.

Charter A written grant which establishes a local government corporation or other institution, and defines its purposes and privileges.

Checks and Balances System of government which maintains balance of power among the branches of the government. Sets limits on the power of each branch. Sets up ways for each branch to correct any misuses of power by the other branches.

Citizen Participation Strategies have greater legitimacy and are easier to implement politically when the citizens served by a governmental entity feel that their interests and issues have been properly addressed during the planning process.

City Council Typical name for the members of a governing body of a municipality.

City Manager The Chief Executive Officer of a municipality.

Civil Relating to the rights of individuals, such as property and personal freedoms. Also, court cases which are not criminal.

Civil Rights Rights which belong to a person because of his or her being a member of a particular society, for example, an American.

Combination Elections A hybrid election system where some candidates are elected on a city-wide basis, while other candidates are elected from a district, or ward.

Committee A group of people officially chosen to investigate or discuss a particular issue.

Compromise To settle differences by accepting less than what was wanted.

Constraint Limitation; restriction.

Contradict To conflict with; to oppose.

Controversial Relating to issues about which people have and express opposing views.

Cost/Benefit Analysis The relationship between economic benefits and costs associated with the operation of the department or program under study. The cost/benefit analysis may include both direct and indirect benefits and costs. Such analysis typically results in a payback period on initial investment.

Cost Center The smallest practical breakdown of expenditure and income into a grouping which will facilitate performance review, service evaluation, and the setting of priorities for a particular activity or service area. Typically, it includes a portion of a single program within a department.

County Manager The Chief Executive Officer of a county government.

Cross-Impact Analysis An analytical technique for identifying the various impacts of specific events or well-defined policy actions on other events. It explores whether the occurrence of one event or implementation of one policy is likely to inhibit, enhance, or have no effect on the occurrence of another event.

Criminal Relating to court cases in which a person has been accused of committing an action that is harmful to the public, such as murder or burglary.

Debate To discuss reasons for and against an issue or idea.

Delegate To grant or assign responsibility to another; to authorize a person or persons to represent the rest of the people.

Direct Democracy The people vote to make all of the decisions about their government.

Discrimination Being treated differently, usually worse, for some characteristic such as race, religion, national origin or sex. Discrimination is discouraged in the U.S.

District Elections An election system where candidates are elected from a district, or ward.

Econometric Model Forecasting technique that involves a system of interdependent regression equations that describe some sector of economic sales or profit activity. The parameters of the regression equations are usually estimated simultaneously. This technique better expresses the casualties involved than an ordinary regression equation.

Effectiveness Performing the right tasks correctly, consistent with a program's mission, goals, and objectives, or work plan. Relates to correctness and accuracy, not the efficiency of the program or tasks performed. Effectiveness alone is not an accurate measure of total productivity.

Efficiency Operating a program or performing work task economically. Relates to dollars spent or saved, not to the effectiveness of the program or task performed. Efficiency alone is not an accurate measure of total productivity.

Elected Officials Those public officials that hold elective office for a specified time period, typically called a term of office.

Environmental Scanning Process of identifying major environmental factors, events, or trends that impact, directly or indirectly, the organization and its internal operating systems. It is one of the initial steps in undertaking a strategic planning process.

Evaluation Systematic review of the mission, goals, objectives, and work plan for the organization and its various components. Evaluation occurs most frequently at the operational level by reviewing organizational objectives. The evaluation process typically results in the preparation of recommendations for needed adjustments.

Executive Person or group of persons responsible for governmental affairs and enforcement of laws.

Executive Director The title frequently used for the Chief Executive Officer of a regional government agency.

Exempt Free or excused from a requirement or duty.

External Environment All relevant elements or forces (for example, social, economic, political, and technological) external to, and having an impact on, the organization and its various components. Includes those forces that are not under the direct control of management.

Forecasting Techniques Methods (for example, qualitative, quantitative, and causal) used to project trends and predict future events or courses of action. Forecasting is an essential component of the strategic planning process. It may be used to analyze the external environment or to project organizational capabilities.

Foreign Policy The way a country treats and relates to the other countries of the world.

Forms of County Government Major forms include Commission, Commission-Administrator, and Council-Executive.

Forms of Municipal Government Major forms include Council-Manager, Mayor-Council, Commission, and Strong Mayor.

General Election A voting process involving most or all areas of the nation or state.

General Purpose Local Governments Includes cities and counties, since they both provide a wide range of services to the citizens they serve.

Gerrymandering Drawing of district lines to maximize the electoral advantage of a political party or faction. The term was first used in 1812, when Elbridge Gerry was Governor of Massachusetts, to characterize the State redistricting plan.

Governor The Chief Executive Officer of a state government.

Hierarchical Ordered by rank or authority.

Hierarchy The order in which authority is ranked.

Impeach To charge a public official with committing a crime.

Inaugurate To place in office by a formal ceremony.

Influence The power to produce or cause an effect; to have an effect upon.
Inherent Rights Essential, basic rights.

Intergovernmental Relations The relationships between public officials at the various levels of government, most often dictated by legislation (e.g., grant requirements).

Internal Environment Relevant elements or forces (e.g., personnel, financial, communications, authority relationships, and management operating systems) internal to, and having an impact on, the operation of the organization and its various components. Includes those forces that are under the direct control of management.

Issue Trend, set of elements, or event which a group decides is important for policy-making purposes.

Issues Management Attempt to manage those issues that are important to an organization. These issues typically surface after the completion of an environmental scanning process, or other practice, leading to the identification of important issues. The issues identified should fall within the scope and purpose of the organization.

Jury A group of people chosen to hear a case in court. The *jury* makes a decision based upon the evidence.

Lame Duck Session A session of Congress meeting after elections have been held, but before the newly elected Congress has convened.

Law In municipal and county government this takes the form of an ordinance, which must be passed by majority vote of the governing body and published in a newspaper of general circulation.

Legislation The act or procedure of making laws; a law or laws made by such a procedure.

Levy To collect, a tax, for example.

Life-Cycle Analysis Involves an analysis and forecasting of new product or service growth rates based on S-curves. The phases of product or service acceptance by various groups are central to this analytical technique.

Line Personnel in those departments charged with responsibility for those functions necessary for the day-to-day performance of the organization. Includes those departments that directly produce goods and/or services to satisfy an organization's marketplace.

Line of Succession Order to succession.

Long-Range Planning Includes a planning process that commences with analyzing the internal organization and projecting current trends into the future for selected organizational components. This planning process may not include an assessment of an organization's external environment. It may be product or service oriented. This term should not be confused with strategic planning.

Management Consists basically of two types—strategic and operational. Strategic management is performed at the top of an organization's hierarchy; everything else is operational management. Operational management is organized along functional lines of responsibility. Strategic management sets direction for the organization, and operational management ensures that this direction is implemented.

Management Information System Integrated information system designed to provide strategic, tactical, and operational information to management. Usually involves periodic written or computer-generated reports which are timely, concise, and meaningful.

Management Operating System Formal system of linkages between different components of the organization by which the various departments communicate with each other and by which management directs the operation and receives information on its performance.

Mayor Typical name for the highest elective office in municipality.

Mission Statement of the role, or purpose, by which an organization plans to serve society. Mission statements may be set for different organizational components or departments. A department usually has only one mission statement.

Municipal The smallest unit of local government in the U.S.

Negotiate To discuss and then compromise on an issue to reach an agreement.

Nonprofit Organization Sometimes referred to as the third sector—the other two being the public and private sectors. Nonprofit organizations generally serve a public purpose and do not generate revenues beyond their operating expenses.

Objectives Tasks which are deemed necessary for an organization, or its components and departments, to achieve its goals. Several detailed objectives are typically set forth for each goal statement. Objectives include the operational implementation of goals.

Operational Issues Issues that relate to the internal operations of an organization such as finance, budgeting, personnel, and technology, to name a few. Operational issues may or may not relate to an organization's external environment and may not be of strategic importance to an organization.

Operational Management Tasks performed by line managers dealing with the operations of the organization. Operational managers may provide input into the formulation of strategic plans, but such plans are formulated by the planning group. Operational managers are key actors in implementing components of strategic plans.

Opponent Person who ran against others in an election for an office or position.

Opportunity Cost Cost of not taking a particular course of action. For example, if there are two issues and one is deemed to be strategic and the other is not, then the opportunity cost is the cost of not pursuing the course of action required for the nonstrategic issue. If the purchase of computers is a strategic issue, and the cost to purchase typewriters is not, then the cost of not acquiring the typewriters is an opportunity cost.

Override To nullify; to pass over.

Pardon To forgive a person for something he/she did wrong; to release or free a person from punishment.

Petition A formal request, usually written, for a right or benefit from a person or group with authority.

Philosophy The general beliefs, attitudes and ideas or theories of a person or group.

Platform The stated principles of a candidate for public office or a political party.

Policy Chosen course of action designed to significantly affect the organization's behavior in prescribed situations.

Political Action Committee (PAC) A group organized to promote its members' views on selected issues, usually through raising money that is contributed to the campaign funds of candidates who support the group's position.

Preliminary Introductory; something that comes before and is necessary to what follows.

Preside To hold the position of authority; to be in charge of a meeting or group.

President The Chief Executive Officer of the federal government organization.

Primary Election Election by which the candidate who will represent a particular political party is chosen.

Productivity Measure of performance that includes the requirements of both efficiency and effectiveness. Includes performing the program or work tasks correctly (effectively) and economically (efficiently).

Pro Tempore For the time being; temporarily.

Ratification Two uses of this term are: (1) the act of approval of a proposed constitutional amendment by the legislatures of the States; (2) the Senate process of advice and consent to treaties negotiated by the President.

Ratify To approve or confirm formally; to make valid and binding.

Redistricting The process within the States of redrawing legislative district boundaries to reflect population changes following the decennial census.

Regional Government A multi-jurisdictional agency that includes any combination of cities and counties, and is usually sub-state in nature. Only a few regional governments involve more than one state.

Regulation Rule or order which controls actions and procedures.

Repeal To take back or recall, usually a law.

Representative Democracy The people choose or elect officials to make decisions for them about their government. On some issues, however, the people vote, rather than their representatives.

Republican Democratic; representative.

Resolution A legislative act without the force of law, such as action taken to adopt a policy or to modify an existing program.

Ruling The official decision of a court on the case being tried.

Sentence Judgment or decision; usually a decision on the punishment for a person convicted of a crime.

Special Purpose Local Governments Includes special districts, which perform a single public service or function (e.g., water, sewer, and transportation districts, to name a few).

Staff Personnel in those departments designed to serve the operating components, or line departments, of an organization (e.g., personnel, finance, general services, purchasing, etc.).

Stakeholder Those individuals, groups, and outside parties that either affect or who are affected by the organization. Examples include constituents, special-interest groups, suppliers, unions, employees, policy-makers, and advisory bodies, to name a few. In any strategic planning process these entities must either be involved or consulted so that their views are given consideration during the planning process.

Strategic Issues Issues included in a strategic plan which are deemed important to the organization and its future performance. These issues may be either internal or external to the organization itself. Typically, external issues are more difficult to manage than internal issues, due to the limited degree of control exercised by public organizations over their outside environment.

Strategic Management Involves setting direction for the organization and typically performed by elected and appointed officials, or some combination of these individuals, once a strategic plan is approved for implementation. While the strategic plan is approved by elected officials, top management is responsible for its administrative implementation.

Strategic Vision Explicit, shared understanding of the nature and purpose of the organization. It specifies what the organization is and should be rather than what it does operationally. The strategic vision is contained within an organization's strategy statement.

Strategy General direction set for the organization and its various components to achieve a desired state in the future. Strategy results from the detailed planning process that assesses the external and internal environment of an organization and results in a work plan that includes mission statements to direct the goals and objectives of the organization.

Structure Segmentation of work into components, typically organized around those goods and services produced, the formal lines of authority and communication between these components, and the information that flows between these communication and authority relationships.

Succession Order in which one person follows another in replacing a person in an office or position.

Table To postpone or delay making a decision on an issue or law.

Time Horizon A timespan included in a plan, or planning document, varies depending on the type of plan being developed. Strategic plans typically have a five or ten year, sometimes longer, time horizon. Operational plans, on the other hand, frequently project a three to five-year timespan into the future.

Unconstitutional In conflict with a constitution.

Veto Power of the head of the executive branch to keep a bill from becoming law.

– – – –

Editor's Note: Some of the above terms were taken from *U.S. Government Structure* (1987) and *Our American Government* (1993), U.S. Government Printing Office, Washington, D.C. Copies of these books may be obtained from the U.S. Government Printing Office, P.O. Box 371954, Pittsburgh, Pennsylvania 15250-7954, or may be ordered over the internet from GPO's online bookstore (http://bookstore.gpo.gov).

B. Local Government Historical Document

(Mecklenburg County was the first local government in America to declare its Independence from Great Britain)

The Mecklenburg Resolution[1]
(May 20, 1775)

I. *Resolved*: That whosoever directly or indirectly abets, or in any way, form, or manner countenances the unchartered and dangerous invasion of our rights, as claimed by Great Britain, is an enemy to this country—to America—and to the inherent and inalienable rights of man.

II. *Resolved*: That we do hereby declare ourselves a free and independent people; are, and of right ought to be a sovereign and self-governing association, under the control of no power, other than that of our God and the General Government of the Congress: To the maintenance of which

Independence we solemnly pledge to each other our mutual cooperation, our Lives, our Fortunes, and our most Sacred Honor.

III. *Resolved*: That as we acknowledge the existence and control of no law or legal officer civil or military, within this county, we do hereby ordain and adopt as a rule of life, all, each, and every one of our former laws, wherein, nevertheless, the Crown of Great Britain never can be considered as holding rights, privileges, or authorities therein.

IV. *Resolved*: That all, each, and every Military Officer in this country is hereby reinstated in his former command and authority, he acting to their regulations, and that every Member present of this Delegation, shall henceforth be a Civil Officer, viz: a Justice of the Peace, in the character of a Committee Man, to issue process, hear and determine all matters of controversy according to said adopted laws, and to preserve Peace, Union, and Harmony in said county, to use every exertion to spread the Love of Country and Fire of Freedom throughout America, until a more general and organized government be established in this Province

ABRAHAM ALEXANDER, *chairman*
JOHN MCKNITT ALEXANDER, *Secretary*

REFERENCE

1   This declaration of independence (with supplementary set of resolutions establishing a form of government) was adopted (as it is claimed) by a convention of delegates from different sections of Mecklenburg County, which assembled at Charlotte May 20, 1775.

C. United States Voting Rights History

(Year, Legislation, Impact)

1776	*Declaration of Independence*	Right to vote during the colonial and Revolutionary periods is restricted to property owners.
1787	*United States Constitution*	States are given the power to regulate their own voting rights.
1856	*State Legislation*	North Carolina is the last state to remove property ownership as a requirement for voting.
1868	*14th Amendment to the U.S. Constitution*	Citizenship is granted to all former slaves. Voters are still defined as male. Voting regulations are still a right of the states.
1870	*15th Amendment to the U.S. Constitution*	It is now law that the right to vote cannot be denied by the federal or state governments based on race.
1887	*Dawes Act*	Citizenship is granted to Native Americans who give up their Tribal affiliations.
1890	*State Constitution*	Wyoming is admitted to statehood and becomes the first state to legislate voting rights for women in its state constitution.
1913	*17th Amendment to the U.S. Constitution*	New law that allows citizens to vote for members of the U.S. Senate, instead of the past practice of having them elected by State Legislatures.
1915	*U.S. Supreme Court Decision*	The U.S. Supreme Court outlawed, in *Guinn v. United States* (Oklahoma), literacy tests for federal elections. The court ruled that this practice was in violation of the 15th Amendment to the U.S. Constitution.
1920	*19th Amendment to the U.S. Constitution*	Women were given the right to vote in both state and federal elections.
1924	*Indian Citizenship*	This law granted all Native Americans the rights of citizenship, including the right to vote in federal elections.
1944	*U.S. Supreme Court Decision*	The U.S. Supreme Court outlawed, in *Smith v. Allwright* (Texas), "white primaries" in Texas and other States. The court ruled that this practice was in violation of the 15th Amendment to the U.S. Constitution.
1957	*Civil Rights Act*	The first law to implement the 15th Amendment to the U.S. Constitution is passed. This law established the Civil Rights Commission, which formally investigates complaints of voter discrimination made by citizens.
1960	*U.S. Supreme Court Decision*	The U.S. Supreme Court, in *Gomillion v. Lightfoot* (Alabama), outlawed the use of "gerrymandering" in election practices. This practice includes boundary determination (or redistricting) changes being made for electoral advantage.
1961	*23rd Amendment to the U.S. Constitution*	Citizens of Washington, D.C., are given the right to vote in presidential elections.

1964	*24th Amendment to the U.S. Constitution*	The right for citizens to vote in federal elections cannot be denied for failure to pay a poll tax.
1965	*Voting Rights Act*	This law forbids states from imposing discriminatory restrictions on the voting rights of citizens, and provides mechanisms to the federal government for the enforcement of this law. This Act was expanded and renewed in 1970, 1975, 1982, and 2006.
1966	*U.S. Supreme Court Decision*	The U.S. Supreme Court, in *Harper v. Virginia Board of Education* (Virginia), eliminated the poll tax as a qualification for voting in any election. This practice was found to be in violation of the 24th Amendment to the U.S. Constitution.
1966	*U.S. Supreme Court Decision*	The U.S. Supreme Court, in *South Carolina v. Katzenbach* (South Carolina), upheld the legality of the Voting Rights Act of 1965.
1970	*U.S. Supreme Court Decision*	The U.S. Supreme Court, in *Oregon v. Mitchell* (Oregon), upheld the ban on the use of literacy tests as a requirement for voting. This ban was made permanent in the 1975 Amendments to the Voting Rights Act.
1971	*26th Amendment to the U.S. Constitution*	The national legal voting age is reduced from 21 years old to 18 years old.
1972	*U.S. Supreme Court Decision*	The U.S. Supreme Court, in *Dunn v. Blumstein* (Tennessee), ruled that lengthy residency requirements for voting in state and local elections are unconstitutional, and suggested a 30-day residency period as being adequate.
1975	*Amendments to the Voting Rights Act*	Mandated that certain voting materials must be printed in languages besides English so that people who do not read English can participate in the voting process.
1993	*National Voter Registration Act*	Attempts to increase the number of eligible citizens who register to vote by making registration available at each state's Department of Motor Vehicles, as well as public assistance and disability agencies.
2002	*Help America Vote Act*	Law requires that states comply with federal mandates for provisional ballots; disability access; centralized, computerized voting lists; electronic voting; and the requirement that first-time voters present identification before they can vote.
2003	*Federal Voting Standards And Procedures Act*	Requires all states to streamline their voter registration process, voting practices, and election procedures.

NOTE

For additional information concerning these documents, and related information, please refer to the *Federal Election Commission,* which is listed in the *National Resource Directory* section of this volume.

D. National Resource Directory

(organized by topics for the public, nonprofit, and educational sectors)

Civic Education

Ackerman Center for Democratic Citizenship
(http://www.education.purdue.edu/ackerman-center/)

American Democracy Project
(http://www.aascu.org/programs/adp/)

Bill of Rights Institute
(https://www.billofrightsinstitute.org/)

Center for Civic Education
(http://www.civiced.org/)

Civic Education Project
(http://www.civiceducationproject.org/)

Civic Renewal Initiative
(http://ncoc.org/civic-renewal-initiative/)

Constitutional Rights Foundation
(http://www.crf-usa.org/)

Kellogg Foundation
(http://www.wkkf.org/)

National Endowment for Democracy
(http://www.ned.org/)

National Institute for Citizen Education in the Law
(https://eric.ed.gov/)

Civil Rights and Civil Liberties

American Civil Liberties Union
(http://www.aclu.org/)

Constitution Society
(https://constitution.org/)

Freedom Forum
(http://www.freedomforum.org/)

Judicial Watch
(https://www.judicialwatch.org/)

League of Women Voters
(http://www.lwv.org/)

National Coalition Against Censorship
(http://www.ncac.org/)

Project Vote Smart
(http://www.vote-smart.org/)

U.S. Commission on Civil Rights
(https://www.usccr.gov/)

Historical

Center for the Study of Federalism
(https://federalism.org)

Center for the Study of the Presidency
(https://www.thepresidency.org/)

Constitution Facts
(http://www.constitutionfacts.com/)

Freedoms Foundation at Valley Forge
(http://www.ffvf.org/)

National Constitution Center
(http://www.constitutioncenter.org/)

Supreme Court Historical Society
(http:www.supremecourthistory.org/)

The Avalon Project
(http://avalon.law.yale.edu/)

White House Historical Association
(http://www.whitehousehistory.org/)

Political Parties

Democratic National Committee
(http://www.democrats.org)

Green Party of the United States
(https://www.gp.org/)

Libertarian Party
(http://www.lp.org/)

Natural Law Party
(https://www.natural-law.org/)

Reform Party
(http://www.reformparty.org/)

Republican National Committee
(http://www.gop.com/)

Socialist Party
(http://www.socialist.org/)

Professional Associations

American Bar Association
(https://www.americanbar.org)

American Planning Association
(https://www.planning.org/)

American Political Science Association
(http://www.apsanet.org/)

American Society for Public Administration
(http://www.aspanet.org/)

Association for Metropolitan Planning
Organizations
(http://www.ampo.org/)

Public Policy

Association for Public Policy Analysis and
Management
(http://www.appam.org/)

National League of Cities
(http://www.nlc.org/)

Secretary of State/State of Connecticut
(http://www.sots.ct.gov/)

U.S. Conference of Mayors
(http://www.usmayors.org/)

Center for Public Policy Alternatives
(https://www.cpparesearch.org/)

Center for Public Integrity
(http://www.publicintegrity.org)

Common Cause
(http://www.commoncause.org/)

National Center for Public Policy Research
(http://www.nationalcenter.org/)

Pew Research Center
(http://pewresearch.org/)

State and Local Government

Council of State Governments
(http://www.csg.org/)

International City/County Management
Association
(http://icma.org/)

Local Government Commission
(http://www.lgc.org/)

National Association of Counties
(http://www.naco.org/)

National Association of Regional Councils
(http://www.narc.org/)

National Association of Towns and Townships
(http://natat.org/)

National Center for State Courts
(http://www.ncsc.org/)

National Civic League
(http://www.ncl.org/)

National Conference of State Legislatures
(http://www.ncsl.org/)

National Governors Association
(http://www.nga.org/)

U.S. Senate
(http://www.senate.gov/)

U.S. Supreme Court
(http://www.supremecourtus.gov/)

White House
(http://www.whitehouse.gov/)

U.S. Government

Federal Communications Commission
(http://www.fcc.gov/)

Federal Election Commission
(http://www.fec.gov/)

Federal Judicial Center
(http://www.fjc.gov/)

Federal Judiciary Homepage
(http://www.uscourts.gov/)

Library of Congress
(http://lcweb.loc.gov/)

National Endowment for the Humanities
(http://www.neh.gov/)

Thomas Legislative Information
(http://www.congress.gov/)

U.S. Census Bureau
(http://www.census.gov/)

U.S. Department of State
(http://www.state.gov)

U.S. Department of the Interior
(http://www.doi.gov/)

U.S. House of Representatives
(http://www.house.gov/)

U.S. National Archives and Records
Administration
(http://www.archives.gov/)

Others

Brookings Institution
(http://www.Brookings.edu/)

Heritage Foundation
(http://www.heritage.org/)

National Humanities Center
(https://nationalhumanitiescenter.org)

National Taxpayers Union
(http://www.ntu.org/)

National Urban League
(http://www.nul.org/)

Smithsonian Institution
(http://www.si.edu/)

Street Law, Inc.
(http://www.streetlaw.org/)

Supreme Court Decisions
(http://law.cornell.edu/supremecourt/text)

United Kingdom Parliamentary Archives
(https://www.parliament.uk/archives/)

Urban Institute
(http://www.urban.org/)

Wikipedia Encyclopedia
(http://www.wikipedia.org/)

NOTE

Some professional associations are listed under headings that fit their primary mission. Those that do not fit into one of the general topics are listed above under "Others."

E. State Municipal League Directory

Most states have a municipal league, which serves as a valuable source of information about city government innovations and programs. Additional information on eminent domain is available from the following state municipal league websites:

Alabama League of Municipalities
(http://www.alalm.org/)

Alaska Municipal League
(http://www.akml.org/)

League of Arizona Cities and Towns
(https://www.azleague.org/)

Arkansas Municipal League
(http://www.arml.org/)

League of California Cities
(http://www.calcities.org/)

Colorado Municipal League
(https://www.cml.org/)

Connecticut Conference of Municipalities
(https://www.ccm-ct.org/)

Delaware League of Local Governments
(https://dllg.delaware.gov)

Florida League of Cities
(https://www.flcities.com)

Georgia Municipal Association
(https://www.gacities.com/)

Association of Idaho Cities
(http://www.idahocities.org/)

Illinois Municipal League
(http://www.iml.org/)

Indiana Association of Cities and Towns
(https://aimindiana.org/)

Iowa League of Cities
(http://www.iowaleague.org/)

New Jersey State League of Municipalities
(http://www.njlm.org/)

New Mexico Municipal League
(www.nmml.org/)

League of Kansas Municipalities
(http://www.lkm.org/)

Kentucky League of Cities, Inc.
(http://www.klc.org/)

Louisiana Municipal Association
(http://www.lma.org/)

Maine Municipal Association
(http://www.memun.org/)

Maryland Municipal League
(http://www.mdmunicipal.org/)

Massachusetts Municipal Association
(http://www.mma.org/)

Michigan Municipal League
(https://www.mml.org/)

League of Minnesota Cities
(http://www.lmc.org/)

Mississippi Municipal League
(http://www.mmlonline.com/)

Missouri Municipal League
(http://www.mocities.com/)

Montana League of Cities and Towns
(https://mtleague.org)

League of Nebraska Municipalities
(http://www.lonm.org/)

Nevada League of Cities and Municipalities
(http://www.nvleague.org/)

New Hampshire Municipal Association
(http://www.nhmunicipal.org/)

South Dakota Municipal League
(http://www.sdmunicipalleague.org/)

Tennessee Municipal League
(http://www.tml1.org)

New York State Conference of Mayors
and Municipal Officials
(http://www.nycom.org/)

North Carolina League of Municipalities
(http://www.nclm.org/)

North Dakota League of Cities
(https://www.ndlc.org/)

Ohio Municipal League
(http://www.omlohio.org/)

Oklahoma Municipal League
(http://www.oml.org/)

League of Oregon Cities
(http://www.orcities.org/)

Pennsylvania Municipal League
(http://www.pml.org/)

Rhode Island League of Cities
And Towns
(http://www.rileague.org/)

Municipal Association of South Carolina
(http://www.masc.sc/)

Texas Municipal League
(http://www.tml.org/)

Utah League of Cities and Towns
(http://www.ulct.org/)

Vermont League of Cities and Towns
(http://www.vlct.org/)

Virginia Municipal League
(http://www.vml.org/)

Association of Washington Cities
(http://www.wacities.org)

West Virginia Municipal League
(http://www.wvml.org/)

League of Wisconsin Municipalities
(https://www.lwm-info.org/)

Wyoming Association of Municipalities
(http://www.wyomuni.org/)

F. State Library Directory

Most state libraries have copies of state laws, both proposed and adopted, in an on-line database. Many states also have copies of the various laws adopted in those cities and towns within their jurisdictions. They are an excellent resource for eminent domain.

Alabama
Alabama Department of Archives & History
(http://archives.state.al.us/)

Alabama Public Library Services
(http://statelibrary.alabama.gov/)

Alaska
Alaska State Library
(http://www.library.alaska.gov/)

Arizona
Arizona Department of Library, Archives and Public Records
(http://www.azlibrary.gov/)

Arkansas
Arkansas State Library
(http://www.asl.lib.ar.us/)

California
California State Library
(http://www.library.ca.gov/)

Colorado
Colorado State Library and Adult Education Office
(http://www.cde.state.co.us/cdelib/)

Colorado Virtual Library
(http://www.coloradovirtuallibrary.org/)

Connecticut
Connecticut State Library
(http://www.ctstatelibrary.org/)

Delaware
Delaware Library Catalog Consortium
(https://lib.de.us/about-us/about-dlc/)

Delaware Division of Libraries
(http://www.libraries.delaware.gov/)

Maine
Maine State Library
(http://www.state.me.us/msl/)

District of Columbia
District of Columbia Public Library
(http://www.dclibrary.org/)

Florida
State Library and Archives of Florida
(http://www.dos.myflorida.com/library-archives)

Georgia
Office of Public Library Services
(http://www.georgialibraries.org/)

Hawaii
Hawaii State Public Library System
(http://www.librarieshawaii.org/)

Idaho
Idaho Commission for Libraries
(http://libraries.idaho.gov/)

Illinois
Illinois State Library
(http://www.cyberdriveillinois.com/services)

Indiana
Indiana State Library
(http://www.in.gov.library/)

Iowa
State Library of Iowa
(http://www.statelibraryofiowa.org/)

Kansas
Kansas State Library
(http://www.kslib.info/)

Kentucky
Kentucky Department for Libraries and Archives
(http:kdla.ky.gov/)

Louisiana
State Library of Louisiana
(http://www.state.lib.la.us/)

New York
The New York State Library
(http://www.nysl.nysed.gov/)

Maryland
Sailor: Maryland's Public Information Network
(http://www.archives.nysed.gov/)

Massachusetts
Massachusetts Board of Library Commissioners
(http://mblc.state.ma.us/)

Michigan
Library of Michigan
(http://www.michigan/gov/libraryofmichigan)

Minnesota
State Government Libraries
(http://www.libraries.state.mn.us/)

Mississippi
Mississippi Library Commission
(http://www.mlc.lib.ms.us/)

Missouri
Missouri State Library
(http://www.sos.mo.gov/library/)

Montana
Montana State Library
(http://www.home.msl.mt.gov/)

Nebraska
Nebraska Library Commission
(http://www.nlc.state.ne.us/)

Nevada
Nevada State Library and Archives
(http://www.nsladigitalcollections.org)

New Hampshire
New Hampshire State Library
(http://www.nh.gov.nhsl/)

New Jersey
The New Jersey State Library
(http://www.njstatelib.org/)

New Mexico
New Mexico State Library
(http://www.nmstatelibrary.org/)

Utah
Utah State Library
(http://library.utah.gov)

Vermont
Vermont Department of Libraries
(http://libraries.vermont.gov/)

New York State Archives
(http://www.sailor.lib.md.us/)

North Carolina
State Library of North Carolina
(https://statelibrary/ncdcr.gov/)

North Dakota
North Dakota State Library
(http://www.library.nd.gov/)

Ohio
State Library of Ohio
(http://www.library.ohio.gov/)

Oklahoma
Oklahoma Department of Libraries
(http://www.odl.state.ok.us/)

Oregon
Oregon State Library
(http:/oregon.gov/OSL/)

Pennsylvania
State Library of Pennsylvania
(https://www.statelibrary.pa.gov/)

Rhode Island
Office of Library and Information Services
(http://www.olis.ri.gov/)

South Carolina
South Carolina State Library
(http://www.statelibrary.sc.gov/)

South Dakota
South Dakota State Library
(http://library.sd.gov/)

Tennessee
Tennessee State Library & Archives
(http://www.tennessee.gov.tsla/)

Texas
Texas State Library and Archives Commission
(http://www.tsl.state.tx.us/)

West Virginia
West Virginia Library Commission
(http://wvlc.lib.wv.us/)

West Virginia Archives and History
(https://www.wvculture.org/history/archivesindex
.aspx)

Virginia
The Library of Virginia
(http://www.lva.virginia.gov/)

Washington
Washington State Library
(http://www.secstate.wa.gov/library/)

Wisconsin
Wisconsin Department of Public Instruction:
Division for Libraries, Technology, and
Community Learning
(http://www.dpi.wi.gov/dltcl/)

Wyoming
Wyoming State Library
(http://www.library.wyo.gov/)

G. Books by Roger L. Kemp

(as author, contributing author, and editor)

(1)   Roger L. Kemp, *Coping with Proposition 13*, Lexington Books, D.C. Heath and Company, Lexington, MA, and Toronto, Canada (1980)

(2)   Roger L. Kemp, "The Administration of Scarcity: Managing Government in Hard Times," *Conferencia De Las Grandes Ciudades De Las America,* Interamerican Foundation of Cities, San Juan, Puerto Rico (1983)

(3)   Roger L. Kemp, *Cutback Management: A Trinational Perspective,* Transaction Books, New Brunswick, NJ, and London, England (1983)

(4)   Roger L. Kemp, *Research in Urban Policy: Coping with Urban Austerity,* JAI Press, Inc., Greenwich, CT, and London, England (1985)

(5)   Roger L. Kemp, *America's Infrastructure: Problems and Prospects,* The Interstate Printers and Publishers, Danville, IL (1986)

(6)   Roger L. Kemp, *Coping with Proposition 13: Strategies for Hard Times,* Robert E. Krieger Publishing Company, Malabar, FL (1988)

(7)   Roger L. Kemp, *America's Cities: Strategic Planning for the Future,* The Interstate Printers and Publishers, Danville, IL (1988)

(8)   Roger L. Kemp, *The Hidden Wealth of Cities: Policy and Productivity Methods for American Local Governments,* JAI Press, Inc., Greenwich, CT, and London, England (1989)

(9)   Roger L. Kemp, *Strategic Planning in Local Government: A Casebook,* Planner's Press, American Planning Association, Chicago, IL, and Washington, D.C. (1992)

(10) Roger L. Kemp, *Strategic Planning for Local Government,* International City/County Management Association, Washington, D.C. (1993)

(11) Roger L. Kemp, *America's Cities: Problems and Prospects,* Avebury Press, Alershot, England (1995)

(12) Roger L. Kemp, *Helping Business – The Library's Role in Community Economic Development, A How-To-Do-It Manual,* Neal-Schuman Publishers, Inc., New York, NY, and London, England (1997)

(13) Roger L. Kemp, *Homeland Security: Best Practices for Local Government,* 1ˢᵗ Edition, International City/County Management Association, Washington, D.C. (2003)

(14) Roger L. Kemp, *Cities and the Arts: A Handbook for Renewal,* McFarland & Company, Inc., Jefferson, NC (2004)

(15) Roger L. Kemp, *Homeland Security Handbook for Citizens and Public Officials,* McFarland & Company, Inc., Jefferson, NC (2006)

(16) Roger L. Kemp, *Main Street Renewal: A Handbook for Citizens and Public Officials,* McFarland & Company, Inc., Jefferson, NC (2006, 2000)

(17) Roger L. Kemp, *Local Government Election Practices: A Handbook for Public Officials and Citizens,* McFarland & Company, Inc., Jefferson, NC (2006, 1999)

(18) Roger L. Kemp, *Cities and Nature: A Handbook for Renewal,* McFarland & Company, Inc., Jefferson, NC (2006)

(19) Roger L. Kemp, *Emergency Management and Homeland Security,* International City/County Management Association, Washington, D.C. (2006)

(20) Roger L. Kemp, *The Inner City: A Handbook for Renewal,* McFarland & Company, Inc., Jefferson, NC (2007, 2001)

(21) Roger L. Kemp, *Privatization: The Provision of Pubic Services by the Private Sector,* McFarland & Company, Inc., Jefferson, NC (2007, 1991)

(22) Roger L. Kemp, *How American Government Works: A Handbook on City, County, Regional, State, and Federal Operations,* McFarland & Company, Inc., Jefferson, NC (2007, 2002)

(23) Roger L. Kemp, *Community Renewal through Municipal Investment: A Handbook for Citizens and Public Officials,* McFarland & Company, Inc., Jefferson, NC (2007, 2003)

(24) Roger L. Kemp, *Regional Government Innovations: A Handbook for Citizens and Public Officials,* McFarland & Company, Inc., Jefferson, NC (2007, 2003)

(25) Roger L. Kemp, *Economic Development in Local Government: A Handbook for Public Officials and Citizens,* McFarland & Company, Inc., Jefferson, NC (2007, 1995)

(26) Roger L. Kemp, *Model Practices for Municipal Governments,* Connecticut Town and City Management Association, University of Connecticut, West Hartford, CT (2007)

(27) Roger L. Kemp, *Managing America's Cities: A Handbook for Local Government Productivity,* McFarland & Company, Inc., Jefferson, NC (2007, 1998)

(28) Roger L. Kemp, *Model Government Charters: A City, County, Regional, State, and Federal Handbook,* McFarland & Company, Inc., Jefferson, NC (2007, 2003)

(29) Roger L. Kemp, *Forms of Local Government: A Handbook on City, County and Regional Options,* McFarland & Company, Inc., Jefferson, NC (2007, 1999)

(30) Roger L. Kemp, *Cities and Cars: A Handbook of Best Practices,* McFarland & Company, Inc., Jefferson, NC (2007)

(31) Roger L. Kemp, *Homeland Security for the Private Sector: A Handbook,* McFarland & Company, Inc., Jefferson, NC (2007)

(32) Roger L. Kemp, *Strategic Planning for Local Government: A Handbook for Officials and Citizens,* McFarland & Company, Inc., Jefferson, NC (2008, 1993)

(33) Roger L. Kemp, *Museums, Libraries and Urban Vitality: A Handbook,* McFarland & Company, Inc., Jefferson, NC (2008)

(34) Roger L. Kemp, *Cities and Growth: A Policy Handbook,* McFarland & Company, Inc., Jefferson, NC (2008)

(35) Roger L. Kemp, *Cities and Sports Stadiums: A Planning Handbook,* McFarland & Company, Inc., Jefferson, NC (2009)

(36) Roger L. Kemp, *Cities and Water: A Handbook for Planning,* McFarland & Company, Inc., Jefferson, NC (2009)

(37) Roger L. Kemp, ***Homeland Security: Best Practices for Local Government,*** 2nd Edition, International City/County Management Association, Washington, D.C. (2010)

(38) Roger L. Kemp, ***Cities and Adult Businesses: A Handbook for Regulatory Planning,*** McFarland & Company, Inc., Jefferson, NC (2010)

(39) Roger L. Kemp, ***Documents of American Democracy: A Collection of Essential Works,*** McFarland & Company, Inc., Jefferson, NC (2010)

(40) Roger L. Kemp, ***Strategies and Technologies for a Sustainable Future,*** World Future Society, Bethesda, MD (2010)

(41) Roger L. Kemp, ***Cities Going Green: A Handbook of Best Practices,*** McFarland & Company, Inc., Jefferson, NC (2011)

(42) Roger L. Kemp, ***The Municipal Budget Crunch: A Handbook for Professionals,*** McFarland & Company, Inc., Jefferson, NC (2012)

(43) Roger L. Kemp, Frank B. Connolly, and Philip K. Schenck, ***Local Government in Connecticut,*** 3rd Edition, Wesleyan University Press, Middletown, CT (2013)

(44) Roger L. Kemp, ***Town and Gown Relations: A Handbook of Best Practices,*** McFarland & Company, Inc., Jefferson, NC (2013)

(45) Roger L. Kemp, ***Global Models of Urban Planning: Best Practices Outside the United States,*** McFarland & Company, Inc., Jefferson, NC (2013)

(46) Roger L. Kemp, ***Urban Transportation Innovations Worldwide: A Handbook of Best Practices Outside the United States,*** McFarland & Company, Inc., Jefferson, NC (2015)

(47) Roger L. Kemp, ***Immigration and America's Cities: A Handbook on Evolving Services,*** McFarland & Company, Inc., Jefferson, NC (2016)

(48) Roger L. Kemp, ***Corruption and American Cities: Essays and Case Studies in Ethical Accountability,*** McFarland & Company, Jefferson, NC (2016)

(49) Roger L. Kemp, ***Privatization in Practice: Reports on Trends, Cases and Debates in Public Service by Business and Nonprofits,*** McFarland & Company, Inc., Jefferson, NC (2016)

(50) Roger L. Kemp, ***Small Town Economic Development: Reports on Growth Strategies in Practice,*** McFarland & Company, Inc., Jefferson, NC (2017)

(51) Roger L. Kemp, Donald F. Norris, Laura Mateczun, Cory Fleming, and Will Fricke, ***Cybersecurity: Protecting Local Government Digital Resources,*** International City/County Management Association, Washington, D.C. (2017)

(52) Roger L. Kemp, ***Eminent Domain and Economic Growth: Perspectives on Benefits, Harms and Trends,*** McFarland & Company, Inc., Jefferson, NC (2018)

(53) Roger L. Kemp, ***Senior Care and Services: Essays and Case Studies on Practices, Innovations and Challenges,*** McFarland & Company, Inc., Jefferson, NC (2019)

(54) Roger L. Kemp, ***Cybersecurity: Current Writings on Threats and Protection,*** McFarland & Company, Inc., Jefferson, NC (2019)

(55) Roger L. Kemp, ***Veteran Care and Services: Essays and Case Studies on Practices, Innovations and Challenges,*** McFarland & Company, Inc., Jefferson, NC (2020)

(56) Roger L. Kemp, *Civics 101 — Poems About America's Cities,* Kindle Direct Publishing, Middletown, DE (2020)

(57) Roger L. Kemp, *Civics 102 — Stories About America's Cities,* AuthorHouse, Bloomington, IN (2021)

(58) Roger L. Kemp, *Civics 103 — Charters That Form America's Governments,* AuthorHouse, Bloomington, IN (2021)

(59) Roger L. Kemp, *Civics 104 — America's Evolving Boundaries,* AuthorHouse, Bloomington, IN (2021)

(60) Roger L. Kemp, *Civics 105 — Documents That Formed America,* AuthorHouse, Bloomington, IN (2021)

(61) Roger L. Kemp, *Civics 106 — Documents That Formed the United Kingdom and the United States,* AuthorHouse, Bloomington, IN (2021)

H. World Travels by Roger L. Kemp

Roger has visited the following countries, and major geographic regions, throughout the world during his public service and consulting career:

- Australia*
- Austria
- Belgium
- Brunei Darussalam
- Canada
- China

- Czech Republic
- Fiji
- France*
- French Polynesia*
- Germany*
- Hong Kong*
- Hungary
- Iceland
- Indonesia*
- Italy*
- Japan*
- Luxembourg*
- Macau
- Malaysia*
- Mexico
- Netherlands
- New Zealand*
- Philippines*
- Puerto Rico*
- Singapore*

- Slovak Republic
- South Korea*
- Switzerland
- Tahiti*
- Thailand

- United Kingdom*
- United States (all regions, and most states)*
- Virgin Islands

* During his visits to many of these locations, Dr. Kemp has met with elected officials, such as a city's Mayor, administrative officers, and department managers. He has also given presentations at several international professional conferences in some of these nations.

I. Some Final Thoughts

Thoughts About America's Cities

El Condor Pasa (If I Could)

I'd rather be a forest than a street.

Yes I would, If I could, I surely would.

I'd rather feel the earth beneath my feet.

Yes I would, If I only could, I surely would.

Simon and Garfunkel, 1970

– – –

America's Livable Cities

Our cities were not designed by city planners,
but by cars, to make the vehicle roadways
and parking spaces available for them.

Our cities must be redesigned by city planners,
to enhance the level of nature within them,
for everyone, especially the citizens who live in our cities.

Roger L. Kemp, 2021

INDEX

Printed in the United States
by Baker & Taylor Publisher Services